Wrestling with the Questions

"Grounded in key moments of the biblical narrative, Gregory Higgins's work helps the reader wrestle with perennial theological questions through engagement with ten major recent theologians, their critics, and supporters. Recognizing that most college students come with little knowledge of the Bible and Christian teachings, his clear, balanced explanations draw the beginner into the discussion."

Bradley Hanson
Director of the Grace Institute for Spiritual Formation, Professor of Religion Emeritus
Luther College, Decorah. Author of *Introduction to Christian Theology* (Fortress, 1997).

Wrestling with the Questions

An Introduction to Contemporary Theologies

Gregory C. Higgins

Fortress Press
Minneapolis

WRESTLING WITH THE QUESTIONS
An Introduction to Contemporary Theologies

Cover image: *Venus* by Nicholas Wilton. © Nicholas Wilton. Used with
permission.
Cover design: Laurie Ingram
Book design: Publication Services
Author photo: Eileen Higgins. Used with permission.

Library of Congress Cataloging-in-Publication Data
Higgins, Gregory C., 1960-
    Wrestling with the questions : an introduction to contemporary
theologies / by Gregory C. Higgins.
        p. cm.
    Includes index.
    ISBN 978-0-8006-6379-7 (alk. paper)
    1. Theology, Doctrinal. I. Title
    BT65.H54   2009
    230'.046—dc22
                        2009003913

The paper used in this publication meets the minimum requirements for
American National Standard for Information Sciences—Permanence of
Paper for Printed Library Materials, ANSI Z329.48–1984.

Manufactured in the U.S.A.

For the living and deceased Christian Brothers (F.S.C.)
of the New York Province

Contents

Introduction

The purpose of this study is to provide college students with an introduction to contemporary Christian theology. It is my hope that this book will meet three specific goals.

First, I hope to acquaint students with some of the leading thinkers and schools of thought within contemporary Christian thought. I have selected ten of the leading thinkers and the movements they represent, but given the rich diversity within current Christian thought, others certainly could have been included. The ten thinkers are all prolific writers, and so for each I have focused almost exclusively on one of his or her texts or a small selection of his or her essays to provide students with a manageable list of readings for study.

Second, an introductory text needs to demonstrate how theology is done to help prepare readers for future study in the field. Whether this future study includes other academic courses, personal reading, or simply thinking about one's own beliefs, an introductory text should provide readers with the tools to help them continue to enrich their theological understanding. In each chapter I focus on one theological question that arises from theological work under consideration and offer some of the assessments other theologians have made of the thinker's argument.

Third, for students who identify themselves as Christians, a theological text should offer some means by which they can better understand the Christian way of life. For Christians, this is the ultimate purpose of studying theology. To that end, the biblical narrative provides the overarching framework for current study. It is the biblical narrative that underlies Christian thought and practice.

As the Lutheran theologian George Lindbeck observes, the scriptural world "supplies the interpretive framework within which believers seek to live their lives and understand reality."[1] The biblical narrative contains countless events and persons, but I focus on ten particular moments: creation, exodus, conquest, exile, restoration, incarnation, crucifixion, resurrection, Pentecost, and the end of time. While arguments certainly could be made to include other moments, I believe there is a general consensus that these ten provide an adequate understanding of the whole of the biblical narrative.

We will, therefore, proceed with our survey of contemporary Christian thought in the following manner. In each chapter, we will highlight one important theological work that is representative of a school of thought within contemporary Christian theology, focus on a theological question raised by that work, and critically evaluate the argument advanced in the text.

An Overview of *Wrestling with the Questions*

In chapter 1, we focus on the biblical claim that humans are created in God's image. The meaning and implications of this essential theological contention have been the source of much debate in feminist Christian circles, and so we concentrate on the argument advanced by Rosemary Radford Ruether (1936–) in her work *Sexism and God-Talk*. Ruether directly confronts the issue of patriarchy in both the biblical writings and the Christian tradition.

In chapter 2, we highlight the plight of the oppressed. Proponents of *liberation theology* insist that a viable contemporary theology needs to address the social, economic, and political inequalities in the world, especially those on the international level. We will examine a foundational work in liberation theology, *A Theology of Liberation: History, Politics, Salvation*, by the Peruvian theologian Gustavo Gutiérrez (1928–).

In chapter 3, we view the problem of social injustice from a unique angle. We examine the problem not from the vantage point of the powerless but rather from that of those who possess the power to effect social change. In the throes of the Depression, the theologian Reinhold Niebuhr (1892–1971), who had recently left his church ministry in Detroit to accept a position at Union Theological Seminary in New York City, published *Moral Man and Immoral Society*. Niebuhr's groundbreaking work combined critical social analysis with an unyielding call for justice. These characteristics would come to define the movement known as *Christian realism*.

In chapter 4, we examine a collection of letters and occasional writings by the jailed German theologian Dietrich Bonhoeffer (1906–1945), who would eventually be hanged by the Nazis for his participation in an assassination plot against Adolf Hitler. Bonhoeffer's *Letters and Papers from Prison* contains his thoughts about, among other things, "a world come of age" that inspired many thinkers in the movement known as *secular theology*.

In chapter 5, theologian Sallie McFague (1933–) addresses the urgent ecological problems that are presently confronting our world and proposes an understanding of God that she believes moves us toward survival, rather than annihilation. To accomplish this, McFague asks us to critically evaluate the received Christian tradition and to revise some of its claims about God, human beings, and the natural world. This approach carries on the long tradition of *liberalism* in Christian thought.

In chapter 6, we deal with one of the leading developments in contemporary Roman Catholic theology. Grounded in the theology of the thirteenth-century theologian Thomas Aquinas, yet conversant with modern philosophy, *Neo-Thomists* offer an analysis of human subjectivity that provides the categories for an understanding of Christ that is relevant to modern Christians. Karl Rahner (1904–1984), whose work we will explore in this chapter, might well be the most influential Catholic theologian of the twentieth century.

In chapter 7, we focus on a modern theology that draws out several implications from the death of Christ for topics ranging from our understanding of God to our involvement in political affairs. In *The Crucified God*, theologian Jürgen Moltmann (1926–) speculates theologically about the provocative question of the effect of the Son's suffering on the Father and develops a political theology based on the meaning of the crucifixion for contemporary Christians.

In chapter 8, we examine the thought of Stanley Hauerwas (1940–). Blazing a new path in the field of contemporary Christian thought, Hauerwas asserts that Christian theology has allowed the assumptions of the wider culture to distract us from the gospel message. In this way, he calls for a postliberal theology that summons us to the way of life preached by Christ and confirmed by his resurrection. The hallmark of this way of life, according to Hauerwas, is a life of Christian nonviolence.

In chapter 9, we address the challenges presented by the conflicting claims of the world's religions. How does Christianity relate to other religions? John Cobb Jr. (1925–) tackles this question in *Christ in a Pluralistic Age* and represents one of the most influential attempts to craft a Christian theology that addresses the radically pluralistic world in which we live.

In chapter 10, we conclude our discussion by considering the end of the world. Is there a final goal for human history? If so, what is the Christian expectation regarding this final state of affairs, and how does this hope impact Christians' understanding of the present? Theologian Wolfhart Pannenberg (1928–) addressed these important questions in the 1983 Ingersoll Lecture on Immortality that he delivered at the Harvard Divinity School. This lecture will be the basis of our exploration of his thought. Such an investigation also requires that we translate biblical claims about the end of the world into categories that are meaningful for contemporary Christians. This endeavor is known as *hermeneutical theology*.

These ten influential theologians have identified some of the critical theological questions of our day and offered proposals for dealing with those questions that have generated a great deal of interest in theological circles. By engaging in a critical study of their work, not only can we gain a greater knowledge of contemporary Christian thought, but we can also formulate our own assessment of their positions and enter into the conversation that is Christian theology.

I wish to acknowledge several people who helped in the preparation of this book. First, I need to thank Kevin Coyne, Eileen Higgins, Joseph Incandela, and James Massa, who read the manuscript for the original work (*The Tapestry of Christian Theology*) and offered their very helpful comments. Second, thanks to Christopher Bellitto of Paulist Press for his editorial guidance on *Tapestry*. Third, I would like to thank Josh Messner, Michael West, and Ross Miller of Fortress Press for all their work in bringing this current project to completion. Lastly, I dedicate this work to the living and deceased Christian Brothers (F.S.C.) of the New York Province (now part of DENA). The Christian Brothers taught me when I was in high school. I have worked with them now for twenty-five years, and they continue to teach me much about Christianity. For that, I am deeply grateful.

◎ Note

1. George A. Lindbeck, *The Nature of Doctrine* (Philadelphia: Westminster Press, 1984), p. 117.

◉ Suggested Readings

For background on contemporary theology, see David F. Ford, ed., *The Modern Theologians*, 2nd ed. (Malden, Mass.: Blackwell, 1997); Stanley J. Grenz and Roger Olson, *20th-Century Theology* (Downers Grove, Ill.: InterVarsity Press, 1992); Gregory Baum, ed., *The Twentieth Century* (Maryknoll, N.Y.: Orbis Books, 1999); Donald W. Muser and Joseph L. Price, eds., *A New Handbook of Christian Theologians* (Nashville, Tenn.: Abingdon Press, 1996); Ed. L. Miller and Stanley J. Grenz, *Fortress Introduction to Contemporary Theologies* (Minneapolis: Fortress Press, 1998); Alister McGrath, *Christian Theology* (Malden, Mass.: Blackwell, 1994); and James Livingston and Francis Schüssler Fiorenza, *Modern Christian Thought*, 2nd ed., vol. 2 (Minneapolis: Fortress Press, 2006).

For a fine example of a theological investigation structured along narrative lines, see Gabriel Fackre, *The Doctrine of Revelation: A Narrative Interpretation* (Grand Rapids, Mich.: Eerdmans, 1997). See also chapter 14 of Clark H. Pinnock, *Tracking the Maze* (San Francisco: Harper & Row, 1990).

Chapter 1

Creation: Rosemary Radford Ruether and Feminist Theology

What does it mean to be human in God's image?

✥*Looking Ahead:*

Rosemary Radford Ruether (1936–) is a Catholic theologian whose feminist theology seeks to uncover, understand, and undo the many forms of oppression—especially sexism—seen in our world. In her theology, Ruether questions the patriarchal nature of traditional theology—that is, theology primarily written by men for men. Notice in her work how this theme is explained and how it informs her strong claims for a theology written by women for women.

The opening chapters of the Bible introduce us to the narrative world that we will explore throughout our present investigation. The theologian Karl Barth once asked, "What sort of house is it to which the Bible is the door? What sort of country is spread before our eyes when we throw the Bible open?"[1] Barth's own reply was that we enter a "strange new world."

The opening chapters of Genesis seem to confirm Barth's suggestion. The Bible opens with a pair of creation stories (1:1–2:4, 2:4-25). In the first, a majestic God creates the world by command alone ("Then God said, 'Let there be light'; and there was light.") in an orderly six-day progression from chaos to order, concluding with a seventh day of rest. In the second story, God is portrayed in a more anthropomorphic fashion. God forms a man from the clay of the earth and plants a garden in Eden. In this garden stand various trees, among them the tree of knowledge of good and evil and, at the center of the garden, the tree of life. God forms the various wild animals, birds, and cattle and completes the creation by forming a woman from the man's rib.

In Genesis 3, the second creation story takes an even stranger turn. A talking serpent tempts the woman to eat the forbidden fruit from the tree of knowledge, and she shares the fruit with the man. In the course of an afternoon stroll through the garden, the Lord learns of the couple's disobedience. After punishing the serpent, the woman, and the man, the Lord banishes them from the garden, denying them access to the tree of life. Cast east of Eden, the man and woman enter an uncertain world of hostility, toil, and death.

In these opening chapters of the Bible, we confront some of the most fundamental questions of human existence: Who is God? Who are we? What is this world in which we live? For nearly two millennia, Christian thinkers have drawn on the available religious, philosophical, scientific, and literary traditions to articulate their understanding of God, humans, and the world. It is fitting, then, that we pair the opening chapters of Genesis with a theologian who has dedicated her professional career to challenging many of the deeply held traditional Christian beliefs about the nature of God, the identity of humans, and the structure of society. Rosemary Radford Ruether's work has generated vigorous debate and passionate responses of both support and opposition. Our study of Ruether's *Sexism and God-Talk* focuses on the question, What does it mean to be human in God's image?

Biography of Rosemary Radford Ruether

Ruether deliberately allows her own academic training and research, personal life experience, and participation in various social causes to direct the course and content of her writings. She was born in 1936. Her father was an Anglican and her mother a Catholic.[2] She attended Scripps College in Claremont, California. Reflecting on her undergraduate experience, Ruether writes, "Those years of education also laid a solid base of historical consciousness, of awareness of the whole Western historical experience and a methodology for expanding that awareness that continues to undergird the way I ask and answer questions."[3]

As Ruether completed her graduate work and began to raise a family with her husband, Herbert, the United States was becoming more deeply involved in the war in Vietnam, and at home the civil rights movement was making strides. The bishops at the Second Vatican Council were updating the beliefs and practices of the Roman Catholic Church, but the controversy concerning the use of artificial contraception continued to spark dissent among church members. The civil rights movement and the process of renewal within the Roman Catholic Church, "the one questioning American society and the other questioning the Catholic church," writes Ruether, "were the matrix in which my theology developed. From my first writings I became concerned with the interconnection between theological ideas and social practice."[4]

In 1965, Ruether joined the faculty of the School of Religion of Howard University in Washington, DC, and "in the late sixties . . . began formal research on attitudes toward women in the Christian tradition."[5] In 1976, Ruether moved to Garrett-Evangelical Seminary near Chicago, where she spent the bulk of her career. She is currently teaching at the Graduate Theological Union in Berkeley, California. Over the course of her career, she has tackled questions of "racism, religious bigotry, especially anti-semitism, sexism, class hierarchy, colonialism, militarism, and ecological damage," but she has earned the reputation of being "the most widely-read and influential articulator of the . . . feminist movement in theology."[6]

Ruether's *Sexism and God-Talk*

The first creation story in Genesis (1:1–2:4) contains one of the most important elements of a Christian *theological anthropology* (a Christian understanding of what it means to be a human person): Humans are created in the image of God. The question, What does it mean to be human created in God's image? serves as the lens through which we examine Ruether's contribution to contemporary theology.

Ruether begins by affirming the traditional Christian view of humanity: Humans are created in the image of God, yet are fallen, sinful creatures.

> Christian theological anthropology recognizes a dual structure in its understanding of humanity. . . . Historically human nature is fallen, distorted, and sinful. Its original and authentic nature and potential have become obscured. The *imago dei,* or image of God, represents this authentic humanity united with God. It is remanifest as Christ to reconnect us with our original humanity. The question for feminist theology is how this theological dualism of *imago dei/*fallen Adam connects with sexual duality, or humanity as male and female.[7]

The nontraditional dimension of Ruether's theology is that the sinful, fallen world is one characterized by patriarchy, by which she "means not only the subordination of females to males, but the whole structure of Father-ruled society: aristocracy over serfs, masters over slaves, kings over subjects, radical overlords over colonized people."[8]

Ruether asserts that the traditional teachings on theological anthropology have perpetuated a distorted, patriarchal vision of human nature. The tendency has been "to correlate femaleness with the lower part of the human nature in a hierarchical scheme of mind over body, reason over passions."[9] Coupled with this is the persistent claim that Eve caused the Fall and that, consequently, women must now bear the punishment for her offense. "Within history," Ruether writes, "woman's subjugation is both the reflection of her inferior nature and the punishment for her responsibility for sin."[10] As a consequence, patriarchy is believed to be "the natural order" or "the will of God."

While the dominant tradition in Christianity has preserved and promoted the patriarchal view of humanity, Ruether sees three marginalized traditions as offering an egalitarian view. First, the *eschatological feminism* of early Christianity, found also in the theology of the Shakers and the Quakers, viewed the church as anticipating the final redemption of humanity and restoration to its original equality. While the larger social world may operate according to patriarchal rules, the church is governed by the countercultural vision of the equality of men and women. Second, *liberal feminism*, which arose during the eighteenth-century Enlightenment, argued for the equal rights of all human beings, regardless of gender. Unlike eschatological feminism, the focus is on transforming the social, political, and economic institutions of this world. Third, the many forms of *romantic feminism* see masculinity and femininity as equal yet complementary dimensions of the human personality.

Ruether argues that we need to find a "creative synthesis" between liberalism and romanticism. She advocates the equality of persons, regardless of gender, race/ethnicity, or class, but hesitates to embrace the view that men and women have equal yet complementary natures. For this reason, Ruether does not fully endorse the use of the category of *androgyny* in some recent feminist writings.

Androgyny has been used in recent feminist thought to express the human nature that all persons share. *Androgyny* refers to possession of both male and females of both halves of the psychic capacities that have been traditionally separated as masculinity and femininity. The word *androgyny* is misleading, however, since it suggests that males and females possess both "masculine" and "feminine" sides to their psychic capacity. The term thus continues to perpetuate the ideas that certain psychic attributes are to be labeled masculine and others are to be labeled feminine and that humans, by integrating these "masculine" and "feminine" sides of themselves, become "androgynous."[11]

All humans, contends Ruether, are called to integrate the rational and relational capacities. "We need to affirm not the confusing concept of androgyny but rather that all humans possess a full and equivalent human nature and personhood, as *male* and *female*."[12] While Ruether stresses the commonality of the essential human nature of both men and women, other thinkers differentiate between women's nature and men's nature.

This debate over whether men and women have different natures is one of the most intriguing elements in the current study of theological anthropology. The theologian Serene Jones poses the question in the following manner: "Is being a 'woman' the product of nature or nurture? Put another way, does 'womanhood' express an inborn, natural female disposition or follow from socially learned behavior?"[13] The nature-nurture debate asks whether our personalities result from nature (our genetic or biological makeup) or nurture (the influence of our family, culture, or personal experience).

Most thinkers would argue that both have a determinative role in our development, but in the context of feminist thought, the question centers on the issue of gender. Is it true to say that women are more nurturing and intuitive than men? If so, is that a result of socialization, evolution, or biology? Do women and men have different psychological dispositions that result in them having fundamentally different views of human relationships, concepts of morality, and approaches in spirituality?

The role of gender in human identity and social roles extends to debates regarding women's ordination in Roman Catholic circles to competing theories of child development in modern psychology. It demonstrates the centrality of the concept of *imago Dei* to Christian thought and practice yet indicates, as well, the wide-ranging importance of the question.

The concept of the *imago Dei* is the basis for Ruether's account of the desired state of affairs toward which women and men should strive. This future state of personal integration and social reconstruction represents the realization of the potential with which humans were originally endowed when they were created in the image of God. Where patriarchy enforces separation between supposedly manly and womanly behavior or social roles, feminism calls for integration: personal or psychic integration of rationality and relationality and social integration that breaks down barriers between men and women. In this way, we reconnect with the *imago Dei* and more fully recapture the human potential intended by God at the creation.[14]

Ruether's Feminist Theology

Ruether describes her theological project as an examination of the interconnection between theological ideas and social practice. In broad terms, Ruether sees ingrained patterns of patriarchal social thought and practice being legitimated by reference to scriptural and traditional sources that themselves express this patriarchy. To break this vicious cycle, theologians working today need to recover ideas that were marginalized or suppressed from mainline Christianity and to reassert the prophetic tradition that challenges the status quo. In this way, they can construct a theology that moves us away from patriarchy to an egalitarian vision for women and men in both the church and the world. An assessment of Ruether's theology requires that we look at both poles in this position: her theological ideas and her social analysis.

Biblical writings are regarded by Christians as reliable means through which God has communicated to them. Many a theological controversy has been spawned over the question of how exactly Scripture conveys God's revelation (literally, the unveiling of God) or in what that revelation consists. Essentially, however, the problem is knowing what comes from God (and therefore should be the standard for Christian belief and action) and what comes from humans (and therefore can be changed). What, then, is Ruether's own understanding of revelation, and how does Scripture function as a source of God's revelation?

Ruether on Revelation and Scripture

Ruether states, "By *revelatory* we mean breakthrough experiences beyond ordinary consciousness that provide interpretive symbols illuminating the whole of life."[15] By this definition, revelation is understood primarily to be experience, not the writings in the Bible or church doctrine. More specifically, revelatory experience consists of breakthrough moments, in which we arrive at a new understanding of our lives.

Scripture and church life function as the customary means though which most Christians connect with that revelatory experience, but Scripture and church life can also block that experience. When this occurs, the idea that is promoted by either the Bible or the church must be reworked. The experience is what is most important. Scripture and church life are primary connections to that Christian revelatory experience, but ultimately, they are subject to reinterpretation or alteration.

Ruether sees recurring episodes in Christian history in which the original revelatory experience is domesticated by the community that transmits it. That community defines its content and saps it of its original power. The history of determining the canon (the list of accepted books of the Bible) illustrates for Ruether this deterioration of revelation into rigid codification. Church teachers and leaders designate which writings are accepted as revelatory and which are considered heretical or less inspired than others. She writes, "In the process the controlling group marginalizes and suppresses other branches of the community, with their texts and lines of interpretation. The winning group declares itself the privileged line of true (orthodox) interpretation. Thus a canon of Scripture is established."[16] In other instances, church members believe their leaders are out of touch with the spirit of the original revelatory experience. This sparks either a reform movement within the community or a drive to break away from the dominant authority.

Given Ruether's insistence that the original revelatory experience can be muted or suppressed by controlling authorities, how can we identify what is truly God's revelation and not human manipulation of God's message? Ruether proposes the following test for discerning God's revelation: "The critical principle of feminist theology is the promotion of the full humanity of women. . . . Theologically speaking, whatever diminishes or denies the full humanity of women must be presumed not to reflect the divine or an authentic relation to the divine."[17] Any church practice or belief that supports patriarchy or domination is judged, therefore, not to be in accordance with the original revelatory experience of liberation and equality.

Ruether applies this norm for revelation to the Bible and is quite willing to concede that not all elements of the biblical tradition are part of the "usable tradition" for contemporary theology. She states a clear preference for the prophetic tradition and its willingness to speak truth to power. Scriptural texts or interpretations that scapegoat women for the existence of evil in the world, that do not promote egalitarian understandings of the human person, or that confine women to certain social roles are to be rejected. "Feminist readings of the Bible can discern a norm within Biblical faith by which the Biblical texts themselves can be criticized. To the extent to which Biblical texts reflect this normative principle, they are regarded as authoritative. On this basis many aspects of the Bible are to be frankly set aside and rejected."[18]

In her address to the American Academy of Religion on the future of feminist theology, Ruether restated many of her theological positions regarding revelation and Scripture, as well as her conviction that contemporary theologians need to continue to address the problem of patriarchy.

> The community of the good news against patriarchy needs the courage of its convictions, the confident trust that they are indeed in communion with the true foundations of reality, the true divine ground of Being, when they struggle against patriarchy, despite all claims of authority. This faith lies first of all not in the Church, its tradition, including Scripture. The patriarchal distortion of all tradition, including Scripture, throws feminist theology back upon the primary intuitions of religious experience itself, namely, the belief in a divine foundation of reality which is ultimately good, which does not wish evil nor create evil, but affirms and upholds our autonomous personhood as women, in whose image we are made.[19]

In this excerpt of Ruether's address, we find a restatement of the priority of revelatory religious experience, the egalitarian vision grounded in the biblical understanding of all humans as created in the image of God, and the need to critically evaluate all appeals to Scripture and tradition for patriarchal presuppositions.

Assessments of Ruether's
Sexism and God-Talk

Ruether's critics charge that her approach does not provide adequate standards by which to judge competing claims of truth. If there is a "patriarchal distortion" in both Scripture and church pronouncements, then is the only remaining reliable source of God's revelation the original revelatory experience? That seems to make the hard work of assessing the truth of a theological statement a highly subjective enterprise. Is this assigning experience more authority than it rightly deserves in the exposition and defense of certain theological positions over others?

The theologians Ed. L. Miller and Stanley Grenz contend the following:

The heart of the debate over feminist theology lies in its appeal to the feminist consciousness as its highest authority, as well as the use of women's experience to determine what is and what is not normative in Scripture and the Christian tradition. Critics fear that if we draw our "critical principle" solely from the consciousness of a particular group—such as women—we have effectively eliminated any other criterion for engaging in self-criticism. As a result, feminist theologians run the risk of merely replacing an old ideology with a new one.[20]

Other critics of Reuther's work fear that the Christian identity of feminist thought is being endangered when experience is given priority over Scripture and tradition. The theologian Linda Hogan voices the following concern:

To what extent can a theologian who gives priority to women's experiences and [practice] over against texts and traditions, considered to be foundational and thereby preeminent, be considered Christian? Would not the identity of Christianity be too fragmented if each group claimed priority for their experiences, over Scripture and tradition, and yet called themselves Christian? Is there not a core which must remain, regardless of experience, if one wishes to call oneself Christian?[21]

Hogan's concerns are a sampling of other similar questions raised by Ruether's approach to revelation and Scripture: Are scriptural teachings and traditional church practices hopelessly patriarchal? If so, what source replaces them in a theology that identifies itself as Christian? Are there some popular scriptural interpretations or church teachings that are only minimally corroded by patriarchy? Should traditions deemed heretical by the early church be incorporated into contemporary theology? Who has the authority to offer definitive and binding judgments on such matters?

The Future of Feminist Christian Theology

The feminist theologian Anne E. Carr identifies three major emphases in contemporary feminist theology. The first is a *"critique of the past,"* including both Scripture and writings of influential Christian thinkers.[22] This would include Old Testament passages placing responsibility for sin squarely on the shoulders of women and New Testament passages that command women to be silent in the churches (1 Corinthians 14:34). There are, as well, a litany of passages from major theologians in the early, medieval, and modern ages that reflect various patriarchal points of view.

"Second on the agenda of Christian feminist theology," writes Carr, "is the *recovery of the lost history of women* in the Christian tradition."[23] The work of the New Testament scholar and feminist theologian Elisabeth Schüssler Fiorenza represents this type of undertaking. In her work *In Memory of Her,* Schüssler Fiorenza takes as her starting point the unnamed woman in the gospel who anoints Jesus in Bethany. Jesus tells his disciples, "Truly I tell you, wherever the good news is proclaimed in the whole world, what she has done will be told in remembrance of her" (Mark 14:9). Despite this pronouncement by Jesus, writes Schüssler Fiorenza, "the woman's prophetic sign-action did not become a part of the gospel knowledge of Christians. Even her name is lost to us. . . . The name of the betrayer is remembered, but the name of the faithful disciple is forgotten because she was a woman."[24]

Carr describes the third task of feminist theology as "*revisioning Christian categories* in ways that takes seriously the equality and experience of women."[25] The central Christian doctrine that is refashioned is the exclusive use of masculine language referring to God. The theologian Elizabeth A. Johnson asserts, "Feminist theological analysis makes clear that the tenacity with which the patriarchal symbol of God is upheld is nothing less than violation of the first commandment of the decalogue, the worship of an idol."[26]

Relating these three tasks to the question of theological anthropology, we can begin to see the specific contributions feminism has made to contemporary theology. In terms of the first task, the theologian Mary Ann Hinsdale writes,

Critique of malestream theological anthropology has been a constant feature of feminist theology since the late 1960s. In terms of a "corrective," feminist theological anthropology has always insisted on more than a remedial inclusion of women in patriarchal theological reflection; rather, it has been concerned to lift up "women's voice" not simply as critic, but as a shaper of theological anthropology.[27]

In terms of the retrieval of lost history, some thinkers turn to marginalized or suppressed traditions about the human person within mainstream Christianity, while others look outside the Christian tradition. This raises the question of how deeply patriarchal Christianity is. Some thinkers have concluded that Christianity is inherently patriarchal and thus no longer identify themselves as Christians. "Other feminists," writes Ruether, "wish to affirm the possibility of feminist theology within the Judeo-Christian tradition. They seek to uncover the more fundamental meaning of concepts of God, Christ, human personhood, and sin and redemption that can criticize the deformation of these concepts as tools of male domination."[28]

The third task of the feminist theologian is to propose new, richer understandings of the Christian message. As the theologian Michelle A. Gonzalez notes,

> For centuries the doctrine of the *imago Dei* has been misinterpreted to benefit male authority and render women subservient in their "defective" humanity. A critical feminist reconstruction counters centuries of misreading the Christian tradition, arguing that both men and women reflect the divine image fully, This theological anthropology presents an egalitarian vision of humanity that reflects the relational, trinitarian God in whose image we were created.[29]

The current discussion within feminist Christian circles concerns what form this theological reconstruction should take.

Conclusion

Ruether insists, "Feminist theology needs to affirm the God of Exodus, of liberation and new being."[30] In the next chapter, we will examine how another theologian,

Gustavo Gutiérrez, also affirms the need for contemporary Christians to heed the call of "the God of Exodus."

◎ Discussion Questions

1. What impact has the feminist movement had on college-age women and men today?

2. What does it mean to say that humans are created in "the image of God"? What does it mean to say that humans are "fallen"?

3. Is Scripture God's revelation? Does Scripture reflect patriarchal patterns of thought? What implications for Christian theology follow from your answer?

4. Do men and women have different natures? Are women by nature more nurturing? Are men by nature more aggressive?

5. What are the strengths and weaknesses of Ruether's theology?

◎ Notes

1. Karl Barth, "The Strange New World within the Bible," in *The Word of God and the Word of Man* (New York: Harper and Brothers, 1957), p. 28.

2. James J. Bacik, *Contemporary Theologians* (Chicago: Thomas More Press, 1989), p. 180.

3. Rosemary Radford Ruether, *Disputed Questions* (Nashville, Tenn.: Abingdon, 1982), pp. 17–18.

4. Rosemary Radford Ruether, "The Development of My Theology," *Religious Studies Review* 15, no. 1 (1989): 1.

5. Ruether, *Disputed Questions*, p. 118.

6. Ed. L. Miller and Stanley J. Grenz, *Fortress Introduction to Contemporary Theology* (Minneapolis: Fortress Press, 1998), p. 162.

7. Rosemary Radford Ruether, *Sexism and God-Talk: Toward a Feminist Theology* (Boston: Beacon Press, 1983), p. 93.

8. Ibid., p. 61.

9. Ibid., p. 93.

10. Ibid., p. 95.

11. Ibid., pp. 110–111.

12. Ibid., p. 111.

13. Serene Jones, *Feminist Theory and Christian Theology* (Minneapolis: Fortress Press, 2000), p. 23.

14. Ruether, *Sexism and God-Talk*, p. 113

15. Ibid., p. 13.

16. Ibid., p. 14.

17. Ibid., pp. 18–19.

18. Ibid., p. 23

19. Rosemary Radford Ruether, "The Future of Feminist Theology in the Academy," *Journal of the American Academy of Religion* 53 (1985): 710.

20. Miller and Grenz, *Contemporary Theology*, p. 175.

21. Linda Hogan, *From Women's Experience to Feminist Theology* (Sheffield, England: Sheffield Academic Press, 1995), p. 107.

22. Anne E. Carr, *Transforming Grace: Christian Tradition and Women's Experience* (San Francisco: Harper & Row, 1988), p. 7. Italics in original.

23. Carr, *Transforming Grace*, p. 8. Italics in original.

24. Elizabeth Schüssler Fiorenza, *In Memory of Her* (New York: Crossroad, 1983), p. xiii.

25. Carr, *Transforming Grace*, p. 8. Italics in original.

26. Elizabeth A. Johnson, *She Who Is: The Mystery of God in Feminist Theological Discourse* (New York: Crossroad, 1992), p. 39.

27. Mary Ann Hinsdale, "Heeding the Voices," in Ann O'Hara Graff, ed., *In the Embrace of God* (Maryknoll, N.Y.: Orbis Books, 1995), p. 23. Italics in original.

28. Rosemary Radford Ruether, "Feminist Theology," in Alan Richardson and John Bowden, eds., *The Westminster Dictionary of Christian Theology* (Philadelphia: Westminster Press, 1983), p. 211.

29. Michelle A. Gonzalez, *Created in God's Image* (Maryknoll, N.Y.: Orbis Books, 2007), p. 168.

30. Ruether, *Sexism and God-Talk*, p. 70.

◎ Suggested Readings

For a short introduction to Christian feminist theology, see Anne M. Clifford, *Introducing Feminist Theology* (Maryknoll, N.Y.: Orbis Books, 2001). For a helpful annotated bibliography, see Natalie K. Watson, *Feminist Theology* (Grand Rapids, Mich.: Wm. B. Eerdmans, 2003). For a discussion of feminist theological anthropology, see Michelle A. Gonzalez, *Created in God's Image* (Maryknoll, N.Y.: Orbis Books, 2007). For a discussion of theological method in feminist theology, see Anne E. Carr, "The New Vision of Feminist Theology," in Catherine Mowry LaCugna, ed., *Freeing Theology* (San Francisco: HarperSanFrancisco, 1993).

For a brief overview of Ruether's theology, see Mary Hembrow Snyder, "Rosemary Radford Ruether," in Donald W. Musser and Joseph L. Price, eds., *A New Handbook of Christian Theologians* (Nashville, Tenn.: Abingdon Press, 1996). For a scholarly engagement with Ruether's theology, see Nicholas John Ansell, *"The Women Will Overcome the Warrior": A Dialogue with the Christian/Feminist Theology of Rosemary Radford Ruether* (Lanham, Md.: University Press of America, 1994). Also helpful is the retrospective on Ruether's theology in *Religious Studies Review* 15, no. 1 (1989).

Chapter 2

Exodus: Gustavo Gutiérrez and Liberation Theology

How does Christian faith relate to socioeconomic conditions?

> ✍ *Looking Ahead*
>
> Gustavo Gutiérrez (1928–) is a Catholic theologian who, as both priest and academic, represents liberation theology through his concern for the poor and his understanding that Scripture and tradition inform a theology committed to biblical reflection and social and political action. In your reading, pay attention to the importance of liberation, or freedom from oppression, in Gutiérrez's theological argument. It is liberation that commits him to question prevailing social and political systems, and to make strong connections between religion and politics.

The book of Genesis takes the reader on the extraordinary odyssey. From its opening chapters about the primeval history—featuring stories of Adam and Eve, Cain and Abel, Noah, and the tower of Babel—the book details the glorious and ignominious moments in the lives of Abraham, Isaac, and Jacob. From the fearful scene of Abraham's near sacrifice of Isaac to the mystical vision of Jacob's ladder, the patriarchs never fail to inspire, anger, or confound the reader. The final cycle of stories in Genesis involve Joseph. We follow his trials and tribulations, from being thrown into a pit by his jealous brothers; to being taken to Egypt, where he is imprisoned on false charges; to being summoned before the Pharaoh, where he is appointed supervisor of the grain distribution program after correctly interpreting Pharaoh's dreams; and finally, to his being reunited with his father and brothers in Egypt.

In the opening verses of Exodus, a significant change of fortune is noted: "Now a new king arose over Egypt, who did not know Joseph" (1:8). The Israelites are enslaved, but God commissions Moses to lead the people forth from slavery and to guide them to a land flowing with milk and honey.

It is this exodus, this divine liberation of the oppressed, that serves as the focal point for our next theological investigation. How does the gospel relate to the lives of those who live in poverty because of political oppression and economic exploitation? What message should be preached from the pulpit? What political actions, if any, should the church fund and support? In short, how does Christian faith relate to socioeconomic conditions?

Biography of Gustavo Gutiérrez

In this chapter, we will examine the role that the exodus plays in Gustavo Gutiérrez's *theology of liberation*. This "father of liberation theology" was born into a poor family in Lima, Peru, in 1928. Early in his premed academic program, he decided on a career as a psychiatrist, but he later felt a call to the priesthood. He studied in Belgium, France, and Italy.

Gutiérrez read the Catholic thinkers whose work would prove so influential at the Second Vatican Council. The council's decrees and declarations intended to renew the Roman Catholic Church (especially its liturgy), to empower the laity to have a more direct and active voice in church governance, to readjust attitudes toward other

Christians and other world religions, and to reevaluate the church's stance toward worldly issues (international development, political processes, economic policies). In 1959, Gutiérrez was ordained to the priesthood and returned to work with the poor in Peru and to teach at the Catholic University of Lima.[1]

With one foot in ministry and the other in the academic world, Gutiérrez sought to unite the two in a theological vision that would cultivate a model of engagement with the world that was both grounded in the current thinking of the Catholic Church and also responsive to the needs of the poor. Gutiérrez's groundbreaking work *A Theology of Liberation*, which first appeared in English translation in 1973, is the literary outcome of his attempt to bridge theory and practice, academic and pastoral worlds, religion and politics, and the old and the new. In many ways, *A Theology of Liberation* is, at the same time, both a traditional and revolutionary work of theology. Gutiérrez grounds his work in both Scripture and the traditional teachings of the Catholic Church, especially the teachings contained in the documents of the Second Vatican Council. He sees in his work a continuity with the teachings found in those sources, yet he also gives voice to a new type of theology emerging from the struggles of the poor in Latin America.

Gutiérrez's *A Theology of Liberation*

Gutiérrez believes his own approach to theology incorporates many of the tasks traditionally assigned to the field of theology yet also moves beyond them. In the early church, Gutiérrez points out, theology was linked to the spiritual life. While often removed from worldly concerns, this spiritual theology consisted, in large part, of meditation on the Bible. In the twelfth century, theology became regarded as a science, as an intellectual discipline that produced wisdom. A product of the union of faith and reason, this wisdom was unfortunately treated by some later theologians as a list of revealed truths to be systematically presented and defended. Such presentations often seemed removed from the struggles of living a Christian life.

Gutiérrez proposes a new understanding of theology as "critical reflection on praxis." He writes, "Theology as a critical reflection on Christian praxis in the light of the Word does not replace the other functions of theology, such as wisdom and rational knowledge; rather it presupposes and needs them."[2] Theology, for Gutiérrez, is "critical" in that it makes judgments—judgments regarding Christians beliefs, theological proposals, as well as economic and social issues.

Theology is also grounded in praxis. As Robert McAfee Brown explains, the word *praxis* "is not quite the equivalent of 'practice.' It points to *the ongoing interplay of reflection and action*. When we act, reflect on the action, and then act in a new way on the basis of our reflection (or when we reflect, and then act, and then reflect in a new way on the basis of our action) we are illustrating praxis."[3] Theology arises out of and contributes to the life of the Christian community and the struggle of all people to be liberated from oppression. Gutiérrez concludes,

> Theology as critical reflection on historical praxis is a liberating theology, a theology of the liberating transformation of the history of humankind and also therefore that part of humankind—gathered into *ecclesia* [church]—which openly confesses Christ. This is a theology which does not stop with reflecting on the world, but rather tries to be part of the process through which the world is transformed.[4]

Gutiérrez contends that all theology, like all politics, is local. More precisely, all theology begins as a local affair of reflecting on the Word of God in a unique set of circumstances existing at a particular time and place, which for Gutiérrez means reflecting on the gospel in light of "the material insufficiency and misery"[5] of the poor in Latin America.

Liberation and Salvation

In this new approach to theology, what meaning does Gutiérrez give to the traditional Christian category of salvation? How does salvation relate to Gutiérrez's discussion of liberation? The theologian David Tombs writes, "[Gutiérrez's] stroke of genius was to show that given the social reality of Latin America the language of liberation offered the best insight into the process of salvation."[6]

Gutiérrez speaks of "three reciprocally interpenetrating levels of meaning of the term *liberation*."[7] Tombs describes them as liberation from exploitation, liberation from fatalism, and liberation from sin. Liberation, in other words, has a material component, a psychological component, and a spiritual component. There is freedom from unjust economic arrangements, freedom from a sense of being dominated by forces beyond our control, and freedom from all that spiritually keeps us from communion with God. Liberation cannot focus exclusively on one element to the exclusion of the other two.

Gutiérrez emphasizes that salvation is not exclusively a matter of an individual's afterlife. He notes, "Salvation is not something otherworldly, in regard to which the present life is merely a test. Salvation—the communion of human beings with God and among themselves—is something which embraces all human reality, transforms it, and leads it to its fullness in Christ."[8] This broadened understanding of salvation includes a similarly expanded understanding of sin. Sin is not merely a personal affair; there are sinful social structures that prevent the communion between God and humanity or between humans and their neighbors. With this expanded understanding of salvation and sin, liberation theologians contend, the Bible now delivers to us a message of liberation.

Liberation as the Central Biblical Theme

The Scriptures speak to us of a God who acts on behalf of the poor to liberate them from oppression. This theme runs throughout the entire Scriptures but is seen most clearly and dramatically in the description of the exodus from Egypt. Robert McAfee Brown notes,

> There are a number of passages that are central to Gustavo's response to the Bible, but his theology is not based on a few proof-text passages, a game everybody can play. The Exodus story, for example is central, but for him the truth that God acts *for* "slaves" and *against* oppressive rulers is not limited to the book of Exodus, but is central to the prophets, the gospels and the epistles. It is "the biblical story."[9]

The exodus account illustrates God's intention for humanity (liberation from all forms of oppression), but this intention was present at the very beginning of creation and stands at the end of history as its final goal.

Gutiérrez writes, "The Bible establishes a close link between creation and salvation. But the link is based on the historical and liberating experience of the Exodus."[10] Creation is the beginning of "the salvific adventure of Yahweh." Gutiérrez continues, "The liberation from Egypt—both a historical fact and at the same time a fertile Biblical theme— enriches this vision and is moreover its true source. The creative act is linked, almost identified with, the act which freed Israel from slavery in Egypt."[11] The exodus not only illuminates the initial act of creation; it also forms the basis of hope for the future.

The exodus figures prominently in the preaching of the prophets. "The Exodus is a favorite theme of the prophets," writes Gutiérrez. "What they retain of it is fundamentally the break with the past and the projection toward the future."[12] The prophets announced a future age characterized by peace, justice, and freedom from oppression. This promise of a future age revealed God's intention for humanity, as begun in the act of creation. What believers expect of the future therefore influences how they act in the present. Believers anticipate God's coming kingdom of peace and justice by eliminating violence and injustice in their society. They act in the present in ways that anticipate the future state of humanity. This way of living in hopeful expectation and active anticipation forms the core of Gutiérrez's vision of the Christian life.

Gutiérrez's Account of the Christian Life

Gutiérrez sees in biblical history a progressive revelation about the nature of God. He writes, "The active presence of God in the midst of his people is a part of the oldest and most enduring Biblical promises."[13] The form this awareness takes, however, evolves throughout the Scriptures.

In the earliest manifestation, the Israelites located this presence in particular places, such as the tent or dwelling place, Mount Sinai, the Ark of the Covenant, and the temple. There emerged in the biblical writings, however, a sense that no temple or earthly structure could contain Yahweh. God dwells everywhere. The prophets added another element in the tradition. Their cry of complaint was lodged against those who participated in the external worship practices of Israel yet had within them a heart of stone. The prophets began to envision an age in which God would be present in the heart of every person. In Christ, these traditions reach their fulfillment. The biblical progressive revelation discloses the truth that Jesus embodied: God's loving presence extends to all people and is encountered in the heart of each individual.

How, then, do we encounter God today? Gutiérrez insists that God's intentions for the human race that are embodied in Christ are seen most clearly in the parable of the final judgment in Matthew 25. The parable teaches us that "the least of these who are members of my family" are our neighbors and that loving our neighbors involves concrete actions of feeding the hungry, giving drink to the thirsty, and so on. It is in these moments that we encounter God. "We find the Lord in our encounters with others, especially the poor, marginated, and exploited ones,"[14] Gutiérrez writes. Moreover, "Our encounter with the Lord occurs in our encounter with others, especially in the encounter with those whose human features have been disfigured by oppression, despoliation, and alienation and who have 'no beauty, no majesty' but are the things 'from which men turn away their eyes' (Isa. 53:2-3)."[15] Given the magnitude of the oppression, despoliation, and alienation, on what does Gutiérrez base his confidence for ultimate victory?

The struggle for liberation in solidarity with the poor requires much from those who have committed themselves to this cause. For this reason, conversion is at the heart of Gutiérrez's vision of the Christian life. "To be converted is to commit oneself to the process of the liberation of the poor and oppressed, to commit oneself lucidly, realistically, and concretely."[16] We must be converted from a life of indifference to a life of faith. Gutiérrez sees this way of life as possessing two defining characteristics: gratitude and joy. Given the oppression and injustice in the world, on what is this joy based? Why not cynicism or despair?

This joy ought not to lessen our commitment to those who live in an unjust world, nor should it lead us to a facile, low-cost conciliation. On the contrary, our joy is paschal, guaranteed by the Spirit (Gal. 5:22; 1 Tim. 1:6; Rom. 14:17); it passes through the conflict with the great ones of this world and through the cross in order to enter into life. This is why we celebrate our joy in the present by recalling the passover of the Lord. To recall Christ is to believe in him. And this celebration is a feast (Apoc. 19:7), a feast of the Christian community, those who explicitly confess Christ to be the Lord of history, the liberator of the oppressed.[17]

In a later work, *We Drink from Our Own Wells*, Gutiérrez returns to this theme of Easter joy:

The daily suffering of the poor and the surrender of their lives in the struggle against the causes of their situation have given new power to the Easter message. The deaths of so many in Latin America, whether anonymous individuals or persons better known, have made possible a deeper understanding of the Lord's resurrection. Joy springs therefore from the hope that death is not the final word of history.[18]

Christian hope, therefore, is grounded in the assurance that the Lord of history raised from the dead a victim of injustice who suffered death on a cross at the hands of the politically powerful. In doing so, God demonstrated definitively that injustice and misery do not have the final word in human history. The final word rests with the liberating God.

Assessments of Gutiérrez's
A Theology of Liberation

In his survey of liberation theology, Deane William Ferm devotes a chapter to the five criticisms typically leveled against liberation theology. The charges are that liberation theologians (1) deemphasize the gospel, (2) overemphasize action and neglect reflection, (3) have politicized the faith, (4) support Marxism, and (5) are in favor of violence.[19] Some of these charges are more typically directed at Gutiérrez than others, but this list provides a fair representation of the charges leveled against Gutiérrez's work.

The first charge is that liberation theologians are actually dealing with social or political theory and simply fitting into it those passages from Scripture that support their revolutionary ideas. Ferm believes Gutiérrez is innocent of this charge. While it is certainly true that any theologian could be charged with reading into the Bible meanings that are congenial to his or her theological positions, acknowledges Ferm, "Gutiérrez grounds his call for the liberation of the oppressed in scripture; he sees the exodus and resurrection events as pivotal points in the action of the liberator God."[20] To evaluate the relevance of this criticism, one might ask whether the theme of liberation is a dominant, continuous theme in the entire Bible or merely one theme among many.

The second charge against liberation theology is that it is not sufficiently reflective. In the pursuit of social and political goals, it is charged, liberation theologians neglect the larger questions of philosophy and theology. Ferm makes the following observation: "The role and significance of the transcendent remains a troubling issue for liberation theologians. Although appreciating their genuine concern over idolatry, the question must still be raised, vis-a-vis some forms of liberation theology, Where is God in all this? What happened to the Lord of history? Is eschatology [the end of history] strictly a human enterprise?"[21] The charge is that Gutiérrez needs to specify with greater precision the relationship between the human struggle to establish a just society, which Gutiérrez regards as a salvific act, and the final salvation of humanity, which is exclusively the work of God. Dennis P. McCann raises the problem in the following way:

> If liberation is "a gift of God," in what sense must it be won in a struggle? As we have seen, this is the major

difficulty in correlating the themes of "salvation" and "liberation." Gutiérrez does, however, provide a rule for interpreting this correlation. In describing the Exodus experience as "paradigmatic," he characterized it as a process governed "by the twofold sign of the overriding will of God and the free and conscious consent of men." But this rule raises as many questions as it answers.[22]

This suggests that liberation theologians may need to do more work in terms of tackling issues such as the proper relationship between human and divine causality, especially as it relates to questions of salvation.

The third criticism is that liberation theologians politicize the Christian faith and reduce liberation to freedom from political, social, or economic oppression. Ferm dismisses this charge as a misreading of Gutiérrez. He contends that "although these [liberation] theologians emphasize political involvement, this does not mean that they reduce the meaning of liberation to its political, economic, and social components. To make this accusation is to misread them. Gustavo Gutiérrez emphasizes the necessary spiritual component of liberation."[23]

The fourth criticism, which is one of the most frequent, alleges that Gutiérrez and other liberation theologians incorporate Marxist terminology and analysis into their theology. Is liberation theology actually Marxism clothed in a theological mantle? Ferm admits that liberation theologians often favor socialism and oppose capitalism. He writes, "This is not really surprising. After all, as many observers agree—regardless of whether or not they are advocates of liberation theology—capitalism and its twin, colonialism (or neocolonialism), have caused many of the social inequalities found throughout the Third World."[24]

Whether it is fair to designate liberation theologians as Marxists is, for Ferm, a more complicated question.

First, there is no clear definition of Marxism. Is someone who supports unions and the minimum wage by definition a socialist? Second, is incorporating Marxist categories into one's social, political, or economic analysis sufficient reason to be labeled a Marxist, or is Marxism part of the marketplace of ideas that twentieth-century Western thinkers had at their disposal? Vatican officials expressed their concern with Gutiérrez's theology in the 1984 "Instruction on Certain Aspects of the 'Theology of Liberation.'" The Congregation for the Doctrine of the Faith in the Vatican expressed concern over the "deviations and risks of deviation, damaging to the faith and to Christian living, that are brought about by certain forms of liberation theology which use, in an insufficiently critical manner, concepts borrowed from currents of Marxist thought."[25] Supporters of liberation theology often make the comparison to Thomas Aquinas's incorporation of Aristotle's philosophy into his theology in the thirteenth century. Aristotle's work was deemed "pagan philosophy" and hence unsuitable for inclusion in Christian writings, but Aquinas found the Greek philosopher's work extremely helpful in explicating Christian belief.

The fifth criticism often follows from the concern over Marxism: Are liberation theologians promoting the class struggle advocated by Marxism? Ferm sees little advocacy for violence in the work of liberation theologians. He also mentions that violence takes many forms and that those who criticize it should oppose the institutionalized violence perpetrated against the poor.

The Future of Latin American Liberation Theology

Gutiérrez's liberation theology is rooted in his Latin American experience, but many of his interpreters have incorporated his ideas into their own struggles for liberation (including black theology, womanist theology, *mujerista* theology). We will limit our attention to the future of Latin American liberation theology.

Pablo Richard identifies seven areas of strength that liberation theologians need to further develop. First and foremost, liberation theologians need to root their work in a deep spirituality. As described by Richard, "Liberating spirituality is the capacity to live, experience, discern, and express God's presence among the oppressed. Liberation theology reflects in a systematic and critical way the God who appears in spirituality. If liberation theology comes to be broken off from its root in spirituality, it loses its purpose and dies as theology."[26]

Richard's second and third areas focus on the need to remain focused on the lived experience of the people in Latin America. The fourth area highlights the essential role of the "ecclesial base community" in the future of liberation theology. The base community is a smaller gathering of Christians who actively participate in the life of the community. "The poor participate by creating a new language, a new symbolism, a new 'rhythm,' new liturgical forms, new prayers, a new reading of the Bible, new ministries, and a new theological reflection."[27]

Fifth, the spiritual practice of reading the Bible in light of the experience of the poor allows readers to hear the cry of the poor, both in the Bible and in the world today. The church must always have a *preferential option for the poor*. As Richard writes, "The poor take possession of the Bible today and read it from the point of view of their own culture, awareness and history."[28] Sixth, Christian churches need to recognize the critical importance of the church in the developing nations of the world. "Christianity must get back to its origins and recover its identity in Third World terms, in terms of the world's poor countries and the poor in all the world."[29]

Lastly, like thinkers in any other discipline, liberation theologians need to systematically present their findings, enter into constructive dialogue with other disciplines, and incorporate their findings into other areas of thought and practice. This, of course, can never be pursued at the expense of the actual practice of living among the poor and reflecting with them on their experience in light of Scripture.

Conclusion

How is the concept of exodus best understood and incorporated into Christian thought and practice? Michael Walzer concludes his work *Exodus and Revolution* with the following observation:

> So pharaonic oppression, deliverance, Sinai, and Canaan are still with us, powerful memories shaping our perceptions of the political world. The "door of hope" is still open; things are not what they might be—even when what they might be isn't totally different from what they are. This is a central theme in Western thought, always present though elaborated in many different ways. We still believe, or many of us do, what Exodus first taught, or what it has commonly been taken to teach, about the meaning and possibility of politics and about its proper form:
>
> — first, that wherever you live, it is probably Egypt;
> — second, that there is a better place, a world more attractive, a promised land;
> — and third, that "the way to the land is through the wilderness." There is no way to get from here to there except by joining together and marching.[30]

In the next chapter, we march on to the promised land, where we will turn our attention from the cries for liberation to the battle cries of conquest. Whereas Gutiérrez addresses the liberation of the powerless, Reinhold Niebuhr addresses how Christians can best exercise the power that they possess.

◉ Discussion Questions

1. What does it mean to be *saved*? Does salvation refer to something that happens to us only after we have died, or is salvation in any way a this-worldly concept?

2. Should the church make statements directly related to the political or economic life of a nation? What is the proper role of the church in terms of its relationship to the government?

3. Does God favor the poor? What did Christ mean when he taught, "Blessed are you who are poor, for yours is the kingdom of God" (Luke 6:20)?

4. In the Bible, how important is the theme of the liberating power of God?

5. Should a church being built today have expensive facilities and ornamentation? Should the money that would have been used for stained glass, for instance, be given to the poor?

◉ Notes

1. James J. Bacik, *Contemporary Theologians* (Chicago: Thomas More Press, 1989), p. 166.

2. Gustavo Gutiérrez, *A Theology of Liberation*. Rev. ed. (Maryknoll, N.Y.: Orbis Books, 1988), p. 11.

3. Robert McAfee Brown, *Gustavo Gutiérrez* (Atlanta: John Knox Press, 1980), pp. 33–34.

4. Gutiérrez, *Theology of Liberation*, p. 12.

5. Ibid., p. 14.

6. David Tombs, *Latin American Liberation Theology* (Boston: Brill Academic, 2002), p. 123.

7. Gutiérrez, *Theology of Liberation*, p. 24.

8. Ibid., p. 85.

9. Brown, *Gustavo Gutiérrez*, p. 58. For a contrasting view, see Jeffrey S. Siker, "Uses of the Bible in the Theology of

Gustavo Gutiérrez: Liberating Scriptures of the Poor," *Biblical Interpretation* 4, no. 1 (1996). Siker argues that the exodus story is not "the crucial biblical story or theme underlying Gutiérrez's liberation theology" (p. 44).

10. Gutiérrez, *Theology of Liberation*, p. 86.

11. Ibid., p. 87.

12. Ibid., p. 93.

13. Ibid., p. 106.

14. Ibid., p. 115.

15. Ibid., p. 116.

16. Ibid., p. 118.

17. Ibid., p. 120.

18. Gustavo Gutiérrez, *We Drink from Our Own Wells* (Maryknoll, N.Y.: Orbis Books, 1984), pp. 117–118.

19. Deane William Ferm, *Third World Liberation Theologies: An Introductory Survey* (Maryknoll, N.Y.: Orbis Books, 1986), chapter 5.

20. Ferm, *Third World Liberation Theologies*, p. 102.

21. Ibid., p. 103.

22. Dennis P. McCann, *Christian Realism and Liberation Theology* (Maryknoll, N.Y.: Orbis Books, 1981), p. 194.

23. Ferm, *Third World Liberation Theologies*, p. 105.

24. Ibid., p. 107.

25. Congregation for the Doctrine of the Faith, "Instruction on Certain Aspects of the 'Theology of Liberation,'" in Alfred Hennelly, S.J., *Liberation Theology in Documentary History* (Maryknoll, N.Y.: Orbis Books, 1990), p. 394. This text also appears in *Origins* 14, no. 13 (1984): 193–204.

26. Pablo Richard, "Liberation Theology: A Difficult but Possible Future," in Marc H. Ellis and Otto Maduro, *The Future of Liberation Theology* (Maryknoll, N.Y.: Orbis Books, 1989), pp. 502–503.

27. Richard, "Liberation Theology," p. 505.

28. Ibid., p. 506.

29. Ibid., p. 508.

30. Michael Walzer, *Exodus and Revolution* (New York: Basic Books, 1985), p. 149.

⊚ Suggested Readings

For a theological reflection on the exodus, see David Tracy, "Exodus: Theological Reflection," in *On Naming the Present* (Maryknoll, N.Y.: Orbis Books, 1994).

Gustavo Gutiérrez's most influential work is *A Theology of Liberation*, rev. ed. (Maryknoll, N.Y.: Orbis Books, 1988). The introduction to the fifteenth anniversary edition of this work is reprinted in Marc H. Ellis and Otto Maduro, eds., *Expanding the View: Gustavo Gutiérrez and the Future of Liberation Theology* (Maryknoll, N.Y.: Orbis Books, 1990). For a presentation of Gutiérrez's spiritual theology, see his work *We Drink from Our Own Wells* (Maryknoll, N.Y.: Orbis Books, 1984).

For an introduction to Gutiérrez's work, see Robert McAfee Brown, *Gustavo Gutiérrez* (Atlanta: John Knox Press, 1980), and Curt Cadorette, *From the Heart of the People: The Theology of Gustavo Gutiérrez* (Oak Park, Ill.: Meyer-Stone Books, 1988). See also the "Introduction" in James B. Nickoloff, ed., *Gustavo Gutiérrez: Essential Writings* (Minneapolis: Fortress Press, 1996). A shorter summary can be found in chapter two of Deane William Ferm, *Third World Liberation Theologies: An Introductory Survey* (Maryknoll, N.Y.: Orbis Books, 1986). A useful resource is Alfred T. Hennelly, ed., *Liberation Theology: A Documentary History* (Maryknoll, N.Y.: Orbis Books, 1990). See also Roger Haight, *An Alternative Vision* (Mahwah, N.J.: Paulist Press, 1985).

Chapter 3

Conquest: Reinhold Niebuhr and Christian Realism

How should Christians employ power in a fallen world?

> ✺ *Looking Ahead:*
>
> Reinhold Niebuhr (1892–1971), a Protestant theologian, who served as a parish minister and later became an academic, represents what is known as Christian realism in his theological approach. Consider that he began his work during the social upheaval during the Great Depression and the two world wars. Look at his theological development, which questioned the abiding differences between the morality of individuals and groups—and how political solutions to ensure social justice were naïve and misplaced, requiring instead a realistic view of the moral possibilities of humans within inmoral societies.

The exodus was an overwhelming experience of emancipation. During the desert sojourn that followed, the Israelites struggled with their new status as liberated · slaves. Fearing for their physical survival, some Israelites clamored for a return to Egypt, where they could take strange comfort in knowing that their slavery also assured them of their fill of bread and meat. Others faced trials of a more spiritual nature. They longed for a god they could see and so celebrated when they saw the golden calf glistening in the sun.

The desert—that place in which the Israelites received the law from God and in which they wandered for forty years for their unfaithfulness—has long been regarded as a place of spiritual tension and testing. As we move from the Torah to the book of Joshua, the Israelites are poised to cross the Jordan River and enter the promised land, the land of Canaan. It is the conquest of that land that next serves as our next point of consideration, as the Israelites exercise brute force to take the city of Jericho and the surrounding region.

The taking of the city of Jericho is one of the most dramatic events in the entire Bible. After sending spies into the city of Jericho, Joshua leads the Israelites into the land of Canaan with a miraculous crossing of the Jordan River that is meant to recall the parting of the Red Sea. Angelic forces gather to assist in the taking of Jericho. God then places the city under the "ban," which consists in nothing less than the total annihilation of all living creatures in the city of Jericho (Joshua 6:21). As the biblical scholar Lawrence Boadt explains,

> The people responsible for carrying on the ancient traditions of the conquest emphasized that the victories came from God and that Joshua and the tribes followed God's directions carefully and always dedicated their military victories as a sacrifice to God in thanksgiving for his aid. This is the terrible custom of the "ban," called in Hebrew a *herem*, in which the Israelites were to slay everyone in the defeated towns. It was practiced to show that Israel put all its trust in God alone during the war and sought nothing for itself.[1]

Modern people are shocked by such brutality, but it is necessary to remember that the ancient world did not share that outlook. Our revulsion today at the brutality of the ban also leads to confusion when the Son of God teaches us to turn the other cheek and pray for our persecutors. It is fitting, therefore, that we pause and reflect on the exercise of power by Christians.

The most prominent twentieth-century theologian who has dealt with the use and abuse of power is Reinhold Niebuhr. After a brief biographical sketch of Niebuhr, we will focus on the question, How should Christians employ power in a fallen world? by considering Niebuhr's *Moral Man and Immoral Society.*

Biography of Reinhold Niebuhr

Reinhold Niebuhr was born in Wright City, Missouri, on June 21, 1892.[2] His mother, Lydia Hosto, was a preacher's daughter, and his father, Gustav, was an ordained minister in the Evangelical Synod (now part of the United Church of Christ). Niebuhr attended Elmhurst College from 1907 to 1910, and in 1912, he enrolled in his father's alma mater, Eden Theological Seminary. After graduating from Eden, Niebuhr studied at the Yale Divinity School for two years, receiving his M.A. in 1915. As Niebuhr would later write, "Family needs (my father had died just before my entrance into Yale) and my boredom with epistemology prompted me to foreswear graduate study and the academic career to which it pointed, and to accept a parish of my denomination in Detroit."[3]

The Detroit experience was, in the words of the theologian Larry Rasmussen, "theologically decisive." Rasmussen writes,

On the anvil of harsh industrial reality in Detroit, the trauma of the First World War, and the onset of the worldwide Depression, Niebuhr tested the alternatives he would find wanting—religious and secular liberalism and Marxism—even when he remained a sobered and reformed liberal and a socialist (albeit one who, beguiled by Franklin Roosevelt, came to embrace a mixed economy and gradualist reform). Detroit kindled the Christian indignation that would fire Niebuhr, as well as the restless quest to theologically illumine the events of the day and thereby render them meaningful. It was the prophet's intensity and clarity that Detroit evoked from Niebuhr—or perhaps better said, invoked, since the signs of volcanic activity were already present. Detroit was Niebuhr's entry into the world of his day.[4]

During his thirteen years in Detroit, Niebuhr was a member and chairman of the mayor's Commission on Interracial Relations, represented the Evangelical Synod at the Federal Council (a Protestant interdenominational group that later merged into the National Council of Churches), spoke frequently at conferences and colleges, and began his career as a prolific writer of articles for a variety of religious and secular journals.[5] It was Niebuhr's contact with the workers in the Ford Motor Company plants, however, that would sear in his mind a lasting impression of the dehumanizing effect of both modern industry and capitalism. As D. R. Davies reports,

> Mr. Seebohm Rowntree, after a visit which he paid to the Ford works, said that it was the nearest thing to hell he had ever seen. That was the aspect of it which impinged on Niebuhr. All this triumph of organization, with its efficient and its alleged benefits to the worker, was a vast mechanism which dehumanized and depersonalized the worker at the same time. It was all built up on the principle of a scientific reduction of physical movement to a minimum and of adapting the worker, the human agent, to the remorseless continuity of the machine. It was the worker, enslaved by the conveyor belt, who paid the price for this in nervous tension.[6]

Niebuhr saw firsthand the inequity in power between owner and worker, the human toll of decisions made at upper levels of corporate management, and the complicity of the church in maintaining the status quo.

Niebuhr's parish ministry also put him in touch with ordinary people involved in the daily struggles of life and faith. Later in his life, Niebuhr described his experience of ministering to two elderly ladies in his congregation shortly after he arrived at his parish. Both were dying. The first woman faced her death with great fear and resentment, and the second woman faced her death with peace. The second woman had both raised a family and worked outside the home to support the family, since her husband suffered periodic bouts of insanity. Then, at a time when she could enjoy the benefits of her labor, she was diagnosed with cancer. Niebuhr later recalled, "I stood weekly at her bedside while she told me what passages of Scripture, what Psalms and what prayers to read to her; most of them expressed gratitude for all the mercies of God which she had received in life. She was particularly grateful for her two daughters and their love; and she faced death with the utmost peace of soul. I relearned the essentials of the Christian faith at the bedside of that nice old soul."[7]

William E. Hordern relates another episode from Niebuhr's ministry that seems to have influenced his theology:

Niebuhr told in his classes a story which no doubt had a considerable effect upon his thought and which illustrates his position. In his Detroit pastorate, while he still held a liberal theology, he was teaching a Sunday-school class about the Sermon on the Mount. Having expounded eloquently upon turning the other cheek, he was challenged by one of the boys in the class. This boy made a living for his widowed mother and family by selling papers. Each day, he said, there was a fight among the newsboys to see which one would get the best corner upon which to sell papers. Was he, as a Christian, to turn the other cheek, allow another boy to take his corner, and thus reduce the support that he could give to his family? Niebuhr found that his theology had no answer.[8]

Niebuhr said he both entered and exited from parish life with reluctance. Nonetheless, in 1928, he accepted an offer from Union Theological Seminary on Broadway at 120th Street in New York City, now known as Reinhold Niebuhr Place.

In fact, Niebuhr's appointment to Union Seminary was not without controversy. The president of Union Seminary, Henry Sloan Coffin, was impressed by Niebuhr's preaching and invited him to join the faculty. A Niebuhr supporter, Sherwood Eddy, had offered to pay Niebuhr's salary, which he did for the first two years of Niebuhr's tenure at Union. Nevertheless, though he would enjoy a long career at Union, Niebuhr's appointment was only narrowly approved by the faculty. Rasmussen reports, "Despite the president's strong endorsement and windfall solution to the money matter, the faculty nonetheless approved Niebuhr's appointment by only one vote. After all, he not only did not hold a Ph.D., he had done no doctoral studies whatsoever; and he was a preacher, not a scholar."[9]

The late 1920s were tumultuous times. In October 1929, the United States was thrust into the Depression. About student life at Union Seminary in the late 1920s and early 1930s, J. King Gordon writes,

For those of us who came to Union in 1929, Niebuhr's apocalyptic lectures in Christian Ethics seemed to be documented by the events headlined in the daily press or encountered in the streets of New York—the Wall Street Crash in October, the reassuring words of Mr. Hoover from the White House, the confident announcement of Mr. John D. Rockefeller Sr. that he and his sons were buying up sound stocks at bargain prices, the lengthening breadlines, the apple sellers on the street corners, the protest meetings of the unemployed in Union Square, broken up by Grover Whalen's club-swinging police.[10]

During this time, Niebuhr was also grappling with theological issues and the adequacy of his training in liberal theology to address the complex realities of life in the modern age. His commitment to pacifism began to waver. Things were changing in his personal life, as well. June Bingham writes, "While Niebuhr was grappling, in the early thirties, with the problems of justice in the collective realm, he was learning a thing or two in the personal realm about the problems of love."[11] In 1930, he met Ursula Keppel-Compton, an Oxford theology graduate and the first woman to be awarded the English Fellow Scholarship at Union. The two were engaged the following spring and married in December 1931.[12]

As described by Rasmussen, in the midst of these changing times, Niebuhr "published the volume that launched his scholarly career and immediately established him both as a formidable thinker and a public intellectual. He wrote *Moral Man and Immoral Society* in the course of one summer, and it has been in print continuously since its publication in 1932."[13]

John Bennett offers this opinion of *Moral Man and Immoral Society*:

This book was landmark. It was the first major attack from within the ranks of liberal Christianity upon the optimistic idealism of the liberalism of that period and upon the dominant faith among intellectuals, especially among social scientists, in a coming rational control of history. In the year 1932 the United States was in the depth of the great Depression and Hitler was close to power in Germany. The results of the First World War seemed to be little more than steps toward another world conflict. It was a dark period of history, and yet the liberal theologians and the people whom Niebuhr likes to call "the wise men" had not really begun to face the depth and the stubbornness of evil in the world.[14]

Niebuhr's *Moral Man and Immoral Society*

Paul Merkley argues that *"Moral Man* is meant to be Niebuhr's parting blast at liberalism."[15] Niebuhr wastes no time firing the first shot. The opening line of the introduction sets forth the central thesis of the work: "The thesis to be elaborated in these pages is that a sharp distinction must be drawn between the moral and social behavior of individuals and of social groups, national, racial, and economic; and that this distinction justifies and necessitates political policies which a purely individualistic ethic must always find embarrassing."[16] In the 1960 preface to the work, Niebuhr reaffirms his conviction of the truth of the book's central thesis: "The central thesis was, and is, that the Liberal Movement, both religious and secular, seemed to be unconscious of the basic difference between the morality of individuals and the morality of collectives, whether races, classes or nation."[17] The passage of time seemed only to further corroborate for Niebuhr the truth of this insight. As Robert McAfee Brown notes, "In a late book, *Man's Nature and His Communities,* Niebuhr commented ruefully, as his recognition of the pervasiveness of human sin deepened, that the thesis of the early book could have been more accurately communicated by the title *The Not So Moral Man in His Less Moral Communities.*"[18]

Niebuhr contends that individuals are able to consider the interests of others, to experience sympathy for others in need, and to cultivate a sense of justice that compels them on occasion to act in the interests of others at the expense of their own self-interests. "But," he argues, "all these achievements are more difficult, if not impossible, for human societies and social groups. In every human group there is less reason to guide and check impulse, less capacity for self-transcendence, less ability to comprehend the needs of others and therefore more unrestrained egoism than the individuals, who compose the group, reveal in their personal relationships."[19] Niebuhr takes to task the liberals, both secular and religious, for failing to truly appreciate the radically dissimilar ways that individuals and groups behave. Because liberals overlook that critical distinction, they fail to see the real causes of social injustice and offer solutions to those problems that are misguided and doomed to failure.

Religious and secular liberals of the nineteenth and early twentieth centuries shared a basic optimism about the human potential. While religious liberals looked to the preacher to unleash this potential, secular liberals pinned their hopes on the teacher. Even so, both believed the hope for a better tomorrow for the human race could be realized if the human spirit was properly directed and motivated. For many Christians who were raised with a liberal faith (Niebuhr included), that outlook died on the battlefields of World War I. For this reason, many speak of 1914 as the beginning of the twentieth century. *Moral Man and Immoral Society* was Niebuhr's attempt to rally the troops to a new cause, a new theological and political outlook, one equipped to deal with the complexities and ambiguities of the modern world.

Niebuhr takes aim at religious moralists who assume that the problems of social injustice will be solved either by developing a greater awareness of these problems or by generating a greater sense of religious goodwill. Niebuhr regards both strategies as equally naive. "What is lacking among all these moralists, whether religious or rational, is an understanding of the brutal character of the behavior of all human collectives, and the power of self-interest and collective egoism in all inter-group relations."[20] Niebuhr's more realistic, hard-nosed approach insists that "when collective power, whether in the form of imperialism or class domination, exploits weakness, it can never be dislodged unless power is raised against it."[21] Social change, in other words, does not result from a more perfect education or a purer religion. Rather, the "relations between groups must . . . always be predominantly political rather than ethical, that is, they will be determined by the proportion of power which each group possesses."[22] In plotting a strategy for social change, Niebuhr prefers to speak of justice, rather than love; to emphasize coercion more than cooperation; to assume selfishness, not selflessness; and to approximate goals, rather than attain them.

The most helpful conceptual tool for realistic social analysis, according to the Niebuhr of *Moral Man*, is Marxism, and it is Marxism that provides the framework for much of Niebuhr's social analysis in the second half of his book. Marxism also made clear the need to dislodge the privileged classes, who strained to maintain their economic clout. According to Niebuhr, "The distinctive feature of the Marxian dream is that the destruction of power is regarded as the prerequisite of its attainment. Equality will be established only through the socialisation of the means of production, that is, through the destruction of private property, wherever private property is social power."[23] Niebuhr further insists that the Marxist "is not cynical but only realistic, in maintaining that disproportion of power in society is the real root of social injustice. We have seen how inevitably social privilege is associated with power, and how ownership of the means of production is the significant power in modern society. The clear recognition of that fact is the greatest ethical contribution which Marxian thought has made to the problem of social life."[24] As we have seen in our earlier discussion of liberation theology, one of the most controversial features of

Marxist thought is the inevitability of the class struggle and the need for violent revolution to effect social change.

Niebuhr's discussion of violence in *Moral Man* signals a complete break with his former commitment to pacifism. In this book, he explicitly rejects the intrinsic immorality of violence and revolution. Niebuhr admits that "Western civilisation will not be ripe for proletarian revolutions for many decades, and may never be ripe for them, unless one further condition of the Marxian prophecy is fulfilled, and that is, that the inevitable imperialism of the capitalistic nations will involve them in further wars on a large scale."[25] For that reason, Niebuhr suggests that justice might have to be secured through political means. If revolution is unlikely, "it would become necessary to abandon the hope of achieving a rational equalitarian social goal, and be content with the expectation of its gradual approximation."[26] Nevertheless, "if violence can be justified at all, its terror must have the tempo of a surgeon's skill and healing must follow quickly upon its wounds."[27]

Niebuhr's suggestion that the use of violence may be necessary to secure a just society is not his final word on pacifism. He takes the offensive and challenges the validity of the pacifists' distinction between violent and nonviolent coercion. Whether coercion is violent or nonviolent, insists Niebuhr, it harms either people or property. For instance, refusing to pay taxes or boycotting certain industries causes harm. Consequently, both violent and nonviolent forms of coercion are forms of aggression. Once the distinction between violent and nonviolent coercion has been obliterated, a strategy using either form of coercion must be crafted to achieve a greater balance of power within society.

Niebuhr concludes *Moral Man* with a call to accept a "frank dualism in morals." He writes, "Such a dualism would have two aspects. It would make a distinction between the moral judgments applied to the self and to others; and it would distinguish between what we can expect of individuals and of groups."[28] Society will act along selfish lines, whereas an individual can transcend his or her selfishness and act according to disinterested motives. The individual strives to love; the society aims to be just. The religious individual may submit to injustice; the social group seeks to throw off its yoke. Any attempt to build a more just society needs to recognize this frank dualism, if it is to respond realistically to the complexities of life in modern society.

Assessments of Niebuhr's *Moral Man and Immoral Society*

We will focus on two of the most common criticisms of Niebuhr's work. The first is that Niebuhr's Christian realism amounts to a defense of the status quo. The second is that Niebuhr's theology is insufficiently developed in certain key areas.

It may seem odd that the radical, Marxist author of *Moral Man* would be accused of supporting the status quo, but this is perhaps the most common criticism of Niebuhr's Christian realism. In the article "Christian Realism: Ideology of the Establishment," Ruben A. Alves writes, "Realism and pragmatism are words dear to American ears, hearts, and brains. If this is so, anyone involved who is involved in social analysis should suspect at once that realism is functional to the system, contributes to its preservation and gives it ideological and theological justification."[29] In an article with an equally provocative title, "Apologist of Power: The Long Shadow of Reinhold Niebuhr's Christian Realism," Bill Kellermann reviews two books about Reinhold Niebuhr: one by Richard Fox and the other by Robert McAfee Brown. Kellermann charges that Niebuhr's position

> means that the morally responsible are to be freed from their arrogant pretensions, but also from the squeamishness that holds them back from the exigencies of, say, military necessity. Fox writes of a telling

description of Niebuhr's import to the inner circle policy-makers of the Kennedy administration: "He helped them maintain faith in themselves as political actors in a troubled—what he termed sinful—world. Stakes were high, enemies were wily, responsibility meant taking risks: Niebuhr taught that 'moral men had to play hard-ball.'" Call it justification.[30]

Stanley Hauerwas and Michael Broadway level a similar charge:

Claims of "realism," such as those of Niebuhr, provide the perfect setting for the development of a severe case of ideological blindness. The eventual convergence of Reinhold Niebuhr's "realism" with accepted doctrine of American foreign policy in the 1950s and 1960s further confirms the suspicion that many theologians had accepted a version of reality that was easily compatible with the views of the dominant groups of society.[31]

Robin W. Lovin defends Niebuhr against the charge that his approach to social problems can be reduced to a systematic defense of the prevailing interests of the social and political elite. Lovin comments on the following observation by Hans Morgenthau: "Reinhold Niebuhr has shown that . . . this relationship between a concealed political reality and a corrupted ethic is the very essence of politics; that, in other words, political ideologies are an inevitable weapon in the struggle for power which all participants must use to a greater or lesser extent."[32] Lovin also offers this conclusion:

Niebuhr was puzzled by this accolade, and he found Morgenthau's analysis one-sided. Ideology is inevitably an element in political controversy, but it is not the only element. The moral ambiguities of politics cannot be neglected, but the terms of moral evaluation are not simply reducible to individual and group interests. The political reality to which Niebuhr wants to be attentive thus includes both the "established norms" and the "factors of self-interest and power" which offer resistance to them.[33]

John C. Bennett's observation may prove helpful, as well. He recalls the debates between Niebuhr and Henry Pitney Van Dusen in the Union Theological Seminary chapel. Bennett writes,

> Dr. Van Dusen felt that Niebuhr put too little stress on moral discipline and the formation of character. I always felt that they talked past each other because they were interested in different things. Dr. Niebuhr was concerned about the sins of the strong who were often too well disciplined. Dr. Van Dusen was concerned about the sins of the weak who were in danger of being lost as persons through lack of discipline.[34]

Niebuhr's theology was geared toward those who held power, rather than those for whom power was a distant dream. As Larry Rasmussen notes,

> He was utterly clear-eyed about the sins of those who, holding power, extend and abuse it, rather than surrender or share it. He was less clear about the social-psychological dynamics of relatively powerless people who must proudly claim power in order to experience pride in a strongly self-affirming, constructive, freeing, life-giving and self-empowering sense.[35]

The second criticism leveled against Niebuhr is that his positions are not sufficiently developed theologically. Two features of Niebuhr's writings contribute to this impression. First, in his "Intellectual Autobiography," Niebuhr disavowed the designation "theologian." He claimed no competence to deal with the "nice points of pure theology." Second, as Larry Rasmussen notes,

> Niebuhr was at his very best in his ability to render a theological interpretation of events as a basis for common action for a wide audience. But precisely because of the audience's diverse beliefs, Niebuhr often cast his case in ways which left his Christian presuppositions and convictions unspoken. His theology was always the controlling framework, but his public discourse did not require knowledge of it, much less assent to it, in order to solicit response.[36]

Because Niebuhr's Christian convictions remained unspoken, critics are quick to cite their absence. Hauerwas complains that "Niebuhr simply provided no place for the church as a political alternative to the ways of nations and empires."[37] Bill Kellermann mentions that "a number of commentators have noticed that Niebuhr had little or no doctrine of the resurrection."[38] Kellermann himself offers this stinging criticism of Niebuhr:

> This is ultimately the theological and political crux of the matter. For all the gifts of Niebuhr's thought—his comprehension of the complex ambiguities of every human decision, his contagious biblical appreciation of irony and paradox, his identification of collective sin, his relentless critique of self-righteousness, and his passion for justice—not to mention his lucid rhetoric and epigrammatic one-liners—he lacks one thing: a faith that begins and ends in divine grace.[39]

Other critics charge that Niebuhr did not sufficiently recognize his own theological liberalism while he was attacking it in others. They insist that Niebuhr consigns Jesus to a place of irrelevance for social ethics; his Jesus is the passive, other-worldly Jesus of liberalism.

Lovin again defends Niebuhr:

In a realistic Christian ethics, biblical resources help us to pick out, among a range of forces that have been clearly differentiated and accurately understood, those that move in directions that are compatible with the hope for justice, and to distinguish them from those which do not. The first task of ethical reflection is to establish the connections between human experience, social fact, and biblical symbol that make those judgments possible.[40]

In other words, biblical and theological concepts play a determinative role in Niebuhr's ethics, even when they are not explicitly stated.

The Future of Christian Realism in Contemporary Theology

The approach to social problems that Niebuhr refines in later writings became known as *Christian realism*. Robin W. Lovin, a sympathetic critic of Niebuhr's work, offers the following assessment: "*Moral Man and Immoral Society* was by all measures a major achievement of modern religious social thought, but the idea of Christian Realism that emerges at the end of its pages lacks the synthetic perspective that Niebuhr's writings as a whole offers to the task of Christian ethics."[41] Even in its nascent stage of development in *Moral Man*, however, Niebuhr's Christian realism struck his liberal colleagues as, in the words of Alan Richardson, an "outpouring of a cynical and perverse spirit, very far removed from the benevolent and sanguine serenity which was held to be the hallmark of a truly Christian mind."[42]

Niebuhr's heirs see in Christian realism a method of assessing situations and plotting strategies that identifies the actual causes and remedies of social injustice. Lovin, for example, offers the following defense:

> The reality in question is the multiplicity of forces that drive the decisions that people actually make in situations of political choice. The desire to reward one's friends and punish one's enemies, convictions about the justice of a cause, the hope to advance one's own interests through the success of one's group or party, the need to demonstrate one's powers over events, and the wish to acquire more of it, fear of the loss of power, fear of the consequences of failure—all of these, and more, shape the responses of individuals and groups to choices about use of public resources and about institutions that serve public purposes. To be "realistic" in this context is, Niebuhr suggests, to take all of these realities into account. None should be overlooked, and each should be assigned a weight that reflects its real effect on the course of events, rather than its place in our own scale of values.[43]

Christian realism continues to appeal to those Christians who view participation in the public arena of politics as an opportunity to secure a more just society through consensus building, power sharing, and the willingness to compromise. As Niebuhr noted in *An Interpretation of Christian Ethics*, "Utopianism must inevitably lead to disillusionment."[44] Christians who seek justice in an imperfect world must always strive to create an ideal society, while realistically knowing that such a goal will never be reached.

Conclusion

Of the many students whose lives were affected by Niebuhr, one of the most famous was a young German student who studied at Union Theological Seminary in

1930–1931 named Dietrich Bonhoeffer. Larry Rasmussen reports that "an important relationship developed, and Bonhoeffer, on a trip largely arranged by Niebuhr, found himself back at Union in 1939, making the most important decision of his life—to return to Germany where, before long, he joined family members and others in the conspiracy to overthrow Hitler."[45] It is that decision to which we will turn in chapter 4.

◎ Discussion Questions

1. Would God have commanded the Israelites to kill all living beings in the city of Jericho? What implications follow from your answer for how we should read the Bible?

2. Was Lord Acton right when he said, "Power tends to corrupt, and absolute power corrupts absolutely"?

3. Do honorable, moral individuals do things in their public roles as government officials or corporate executives that they would never do in their private lives?

4. Offer your assessment of one of Niebuhr's most famous lines: "Man's capacity for justice makes democracy possible; but man's inclination to injustice makes democracy necessary" (from *The Children of Light and the Children of Darkness* [New York: Charles Scribner's Sons, 1944], p. xiii).

5. Is nonviolent protest morally superior to violent protest? Why or why not? If taking violent action would produce a more just society, should Christians endorse violence action?

6. How relevant are Jesus' teachings to the complexities of modern life?

7. Could a prolife Christian vote for a prochoice candidate who endorses every other cause that the voter supports?

◉ Notes

1. Lawrence Boadt, *Reading the Old Testament* (Mahwah, N.J.: Paulist Press, 1984), p. 197.

2. For biographical information on Niebuhr, I am relying on Dennis P. McCann, *Christian Realism and Liberation Theology* (Maryknoll, N.Y.: Orbis Books, 1981), chapter 1; and Stanley J. Grenz and Roger E. Olson, *Twentieth-Century Theology* (Downers Grove, Ill.: InterVarsity Press, 1992), pp. 99–101.

3. Reinhold Niebuhr, "Intellectual Autobiography," in *Reinhold Niebuhr: His Religious, Social, and Political Thought*, ed. Charles W. Kegley (New York: Pilgrim Press, 1984), p. 4.

4. Larry Rasmussen, "Introduction," in *Reinhold Niebuhr: Theologian of the Public Life* (London: Collins, 1989), p. 7.

5. See Donald B. Meyer, *The Protestant Search for Political Realism, 1919–1941* (Berkeley: University of California Press, 1960), p. 218.

6. D. R. Davies, *Reinhold Niebuhr: Prophet from America* (New York: Macmillan, 1968), pp. 18–19.

7. Niebuhr, "Intellectual Autobiography," p. 6.

8. William E. Hordern, *A Layman's Guide to Protestant Theology* (New York: Macmillan, 1968), p. 161.

9. Rasmussen, "Introduction," p. 9.

10. Larry Rasmussen, *Reinhold Niebuhr: Theologian of the Public Life* (London: Collins, 1989), p. 287, n. 21.

11. June Bingham, *Courage to Change* (New York: Charles Scribner's Sons, 1972), p. 182.

12. See Rasmussen, "Introduction," p. 12.

13. Ibid., p. 10.

14. John C. Bennett, "The Contribution of Reinhold Niebuhr," *Union Seminary Quarterly Review* 24, no. 1 (1968): 6–7.

15. Paul Merkley, *Reinhold Niebuhr: A Political Account* (Montreal: McGill-Queen's University Press, 1975), p. 83.

16. Reinhold Niebuhr, *Moral Man and Immoral Society* (1932; repr. New York: Charles Scribner's Sons, 1960), p. xi.

17. Ibid., p. ix.

18. Robert McAfee Brown, *The Essential Reinhold Niebuhr* (New Haven, Conn.: Yale University Press, 1986), p. xv.

19. Niebuhr, *Moral Man*, pp. xi–xii.

20. Ibid., p. xx.

21. Ibid., p. xii.

22. Ibid., p. xxiii.
23. Ibid., p. 163.
24. Ibid., p. 163.
25. Ibid., p. 190.
26. Ibid., p. 219.
27. Ibid., p. 220.
28. Ibid., p 271.
29. Ruben A. Alves, "Christian Realism: Ideology of the Establishment," *Christianity and Crisis* 33 (September 17, 1973): 176.
30. Bill Kellermann, "Apologist of Power: The Long Shadow of Reinhold Niebuhr's Christian Realism," *Sojourners* (March 1987): 17.
31. Stanley M. Hauerwas with Michael Broadway, "The Irony of Reinhold Niebuhr: The Ideological Character of Christian Realism," in *Wilderness Wanderings* (Boulder, Colo.: Westview Press, 1997), p. 50.
32. Hans Morgenthau, "The Influence of Reinhold Niebuhr in American Political Life and Thought," in *Reinhold Niebuhr: A Prophetic Voice in Our Time* (Greenwich, Conn.: Seabury Press, 1962), pp. 108–109.
33. Robin W. Lovin, *Reinhold Niebuhr and Christian Realism* (Cambridge: Cambridge University Press, 1995), p. 10.
34. Bennett, "Contribution of Reinhold Niebuhr," p. 11.
35. Larry Rasmussen, "Niebuhr on Power: Assessment and Critique," in Gary A. Gaudin and Douglas John Hall, eds., *Reinhold Niebuhr (1892–1971): A Centenary Appraisal* (Atlanta: Scholars Press, 1984), p. 175.
36. Rasmussen, "Introduction," p. 3.
37. Stanley Hauerwas, *Against the Nations* (San Francisco: Harper & Row, 1985), p. 123.
38. Kellermann, "Apologist of Power," p. 18.
39. Ibid., p. 20.
40. Lovin, *Reinhold Niebuhr and Christian Realism*, p. 105.
41. Ibid., p. 98.
42. Alan Richardson, "Reinhold Niebuhr as Apologist," in Charles E. Kegley, ed., *Reinhold Niebuhr: His Religious, Social, and Political Thought* (New York: Pilgrim Press, 1984), p. 218. Quoted in Nathan A. Scott Jr. "Introduction," *The Legacy of Reinhold Niebuhr* (Chicago: University of Chicago Press, 1975), p. xiii.
43. Lovin, *Reinhold Niebuhr and Christian Realism*, p. 4.

44. Reinhold Niebuhr, *An Interpretation of Christian Ethics* (1935; repr., New York: Seabury Press, 1979), p. 11.

45. Rasmussen, "Introduction," p. 12.

⊚ Suggested Readings

For a biography of Niebuhr, see Richard Wightman Fox, *Reinhold Niebuhr: A Biography* (New York: Pantheon Books, 1985).

For a short introduction to Niebuhr's thought, see any of the following: Larry Rasmussen, "Introduction" to *Reinhold Niebuhr: Theologian of Public Life* (London: Collins, 1989); Nathan A. Scott Jr., ed., "Introduction" to *The Legacy of Reinhold Niebuhr* (Chicago: University of Chicago Press, 1975); chapter 6 of James C. Livingston and Francis Schüssler Fiorenza, *Modern Christian Thought*, 2nd ed., Vol. 2 (Minneapolis: Fortress Press, 2006).

For a longer critical introduction, see either of the following: Robin W. Lovin, *Reinhold Niebuhr and Christian Realism* (Cambridge: Cambridge University Press, 1995); Dennis P. McCann, *Christian Realism and Liberation Theology* (Maryknoll, N.Y.: Orbis Books, 1981).

For discussions of Niebuhr's view of power, see Kenneth Durkin, *Reinhold Niebuhr* (Harrisburg, Pa.: Morehouse, 1989), pp. 41–50; Langdon Gilkey, "Reinhold Niebuhr as Political Theologian," in Richard Harries, ed., *Reinhold Niebuhr and the Issues of Our Time* (Grand Rapids, Mich.: Eerdmans, 1986); and Larry Rasmussen, "Niebuhr's Theory of Power: Social Power and Its Redemption," in Gary A. Gaudin and Douglas John Hall, eds., *Reinhold Niebuhr (1892–1971): A Centenary Appraisal* (Atlanta: Scholars Press, 1984).

For an interesting reflection on the significance of *Moral Man and Immoral Society*, see Matthew Berke, "A Century of Books: An Anniversary Symposium," in *First Things*, March 2000, pp. 41–42.

For interesting discussions of Niebuhr and Christian realism, see Charles T. Mathewes, "Reading Reinhold Niebuhr against Himself," in *The Annual of the Society of Christian Ethics* 19 (1999): 69–94; and Robin W. Lovin, "Christian Realism: A Legacy and a Future," in *The Annual of the Society of Christian Ethics* 20 (2000): 3–18.

Chapter 4

Exile: Dietrich Bonhoeffer and Secular Theology

Is God present in the world?

✤*Looking Ahead*

Dietrich Bonhoeffer (1906–1945) was a German theologian whose work represents secular theology. His theology is informed by the horrible atrocities that took place in his native Germany during World War II. These personal experiences, including a two-year imprisonment in Germany, are revealed in the kinds of theological questions he poses, notably whether or how God may be present in our "secular" world.

The conquest did not secure permanent possession of the promised land for the Israelites. After settling in the land, the twelve tribes slowly moved from a loose confederation to a unified nation under a single monarch, centered around a single religious sanctuary (the temple in Jerusalem). Tribal loyalties, however, simmered underneath the surface, and in 922 BCE, after the death of Solomon, those tensions erupted. The result was a divided nation: a northern kingdom comprised of ten tribes, known collectively as Israel, and a southern kingdom comprised of two tribes, known collectively as Judah.

Although politically and economically the stronger of the two kingdoms, Israel was no match for the armies of the

Assyrian Empire. In a fatal political misjudgment, the last Israelite king refused to pay the annual tribute to Assyria. The Assyrian response was swift and sure: In 721 BCE, the Israelite capital city of Samaria fell and its inhabitants were deported. The Babylonians would eventually succeed the Assyrians as the overlords of Palestine, and the results for Judah would be remarkably similar to those experienced by Israel.

Sensing a weakness in the Babylonian resolve following a difficult battle with the Egyptians, the king of Judah refused to pay the tribute to the Babylonians. The Babylonians responded by raiding the temple and the royal treasuries and exiling many of the leading citizens of Jerusalem to Babylon in 597 BCE. Ten years later, after more political miscalculation, the unthinkable happened: In 587 BCE, the Babylonians burned the temple to the ground and exiled many of the remaining inhabitants to Babylon.

The Babylonians destroyed more than the temple. They shattered the religious, political, and social world of God's chosen people. As John Bright observes,

The destruction of Jerusalem and the subsequent exile mark the great watershed of Israel's history. At a stroke her national existence was ended and, with it, all the institutions in which her corporate life had expressed itself; they would never be re-created in precisely the same form again. The state destroyed and the state cult perforce suspended, the old national-cultic community was broken, and Israel was left for the moment an agglomeration of uprooted and beaten individuals, by no external mark any longer a people. The marvel is that her history did not end altogether. Nevertheless, Israel survived the calamity and, forming a new community out of the wreckage of the old, resumed her life as a people. Her faith, disciplined and strengthened, likewise survived and gradually found the direction that it would follow through all the centuries to come. In the exile and beyond it, Judaism was born.[1]

Out of the exile, new life emerged, as foretold by the prophet Ezekiel in his famous vision of the dry bones (Ezekiel 37). Judaism was born, but first came the horror, the dislocation, and the questioning.

Jews in the twentieth century experienced their own horror, dislocation, and questioning. The haunting images of emaciated faces peering from the crowded bunks of the concentration camps and film footage of mass burials for those exterminated by their captors stand as horrific reminders to modern Jews of the enduring threat of anti-Semitism. For modern Christians, too, questions abound. As John Gager writes, "The experience of the Holocaust reintroduced with unprecedented urgency the question of Christianity's responsibility for anti-Semitism: not simply whether individual Christians had added fuel to modern European anti-Semitism, but whether Christianity itself was, in its essence and from its beginnings, the primary source of anti-Semitism in Western culture."[2]

One theologian who struggled with questions such as these was a young German pastor named Dietrich Bonhoeffer, who would be executed by the Nazis on April 9, 1945.[3] After a brief overview of Bonhoeffer's life, we will turn our attention to the question, Is God present in the world? by examining the central themes in Bonhoeffer's letters from prison. We will conclude with an investigation of the spirituality suggested by Bonhoeffer's provocative aphorisms.

Biography of Dietrich Bonhoeffer

Dietrich Bonhoeffer was born into a comfortable upper-middle-class family in Breslau, Germany, on February 4, 1906. His father was a prominent physician and eventually became professor of psychiatry at the University of Berlin;

his mother was a descendant of August van Huse, a distinguished nineteenth-century German church historian.

After completing his university studies, Bonhoeffer served a German-speaking congregation in Barcelona, Spain. Returning in 1929 to Berlin, he began work on his inaugural dissertation, which was required for securing a faculty position in theology. In 1930, after writing *Act and Being: Transcendental Philosophy and Ontology in Systematic Theology*, Bonhoeffer was given a position teaching systematic theology.[4] Before beginning his teaching career, however, he attended Union Theological Seminary in New York for one year, where he struck up a friendship with Reinhold Niebuhr. In 1931, Bonhoeffer returned to Germany. In addition to his teaching responsibilities, Bonhoeffer continued his ministry and became involved in the ecumenical movement.

The Nazis' rise to power in Germany in 1932 was the first of a series of events that culminated in Bonhoeffer's death at age thirty-nine. The young preacher delivered a radio address in early 1933 that the Nazis cut off before its completion. At that time, the Protestant churches in Germany were divided over the question of loyalty to Adolf Hitler. Some supported the nationalism of the Nazis; they became known as the "German Christians." Others protested what they saw as a threat to church independence; they became known as the "Confessing Church."

In the fall of 1933, Bonhoeffer moved to London to serve as the minister of two German-speaking congregations. There, he met G. K. A. Bell, the Bishop of Chichester, who would play a critical role in a decisive moment later in Bonhoeffer's life. In 1935, Bonhoeffer returned to Germany to head an illegal seminary for the Confessing Church. Despite the Nazi prohibition against the ordination of ministers for the Confessing Church, Bonhoeffer organized a seminary, first in Zingst and then in Finkenwalde near Stettin. In 1936, he was no longer permitted to teach at the

University of Berlin, and in 1937, the Gestapo closed down the seminary.

In 1939, Bonhoeffer accepted an invitation by Reinhold Niebuhr to conduct a lecture tour in the United States. He stayed in the United States for less than a month and returned to Germany. His reasoning was simple: "I must live through this difficult period of our national history with the Christian people of Germany. I will have no right to participate in the reconstruction of Christian life in Germany after the war if I do not share the trials of this time with my people."[5]

Upon his return, Bonhoeffer was forbidden to preach. As described by Geffrey B. Kelly, "Convinced now that submission to the state in the name of conscience unsullied by violence made one an accomplice in the 'great masquerade of evil,' [Bonhoeffer] decided to join the anti-Nazi underground. Its center was the *Abwehr*, the German military intelligence organization."[6] His job was ostensibly to gather intelligence through his ecumenical contacts. His position, however, exempted him from the draft and provided him with ample opportunities to leave the country.

Franklin Sherman reports on one of Bonhoeffer's encounters while in the underground:

At a fateful meeting with the Bishop of Chichester at Sigtuna, Sweden, in May, 1942, Bonhoeffer presented to the bishop for conveyance to the British government detailed information on the plans for overthrowing the Nazi regime, together with proposals for the subsequent establishment of peace. The proposals reached British foreign secretary Anthony Eden but were summarily rejected; "unconditional surrender" was to be the Allied policy.[7]

On April 5, 1943, three months after Bonhoeffer's engagement to Maria von Wedemeyer, two men from the Gestapo arrived at his house and brought him to Tegel Military Prison in Berlin, where he would spend the next eighteen months. During his confinement, he read voraciously and wrote numerous letters to his parents, fiancée, and friends and to the husband of his niece, Eberhard Bethge. These letters, smuggled out of Tegel Prison and hidden by Bethge in tin cans buried in his garden, eventually were published under the title *Letters and Papers from Prison*.

In July 1944, an attempt to assassinate Hitler failed, and the Gestapo's discovery of the secret files of the *Abwehr* in Zossen in September 1944 confirmed Bonhoeffer's role in the assassination plot. He was soon transferred from Tegel to a Gestapo prison on Prinz Albrecht Street, where he was tortured. In February 1945, he was removed to Buchenwald and then to Flossenburg. There, he was court martialled and later hanged on April 9, 1945, just days before Allied forces liberated the camp.

Dietrich Bonhoeffer's life and theology testify to the ongoing relevance of exile as a category of Christian experience. First, he was physically exiled from his native land. An unwelcome prophet, he put himself in self-imposed exile in London and then briefly in the United States. His estrangement, however, was not merely geographical. Bonhoeffer was an exile culturally, as well. He experienced a profound sense of disconnection with the prevailing attitudes of the German nation. Describing Bonhoeffer's growing sense of alienation during the early years of the Third Reich, Eberhard Bethge comments,

> Bonhoeffer's initial position placed him in a difficult dilemma. His personal vitality, the sense of public responsibility which he had inherited, combined with his successful start in an academic career, made it impossible for him simply to submerge silently. If there was no prospect of his still belonging to that society in which he lived, then he had to find a suitable form of

exile. Although the term "inner exile" does not completely cover the phenomenon, it would still be fairly accurate to apply it to Bonhoeffer's passage into the Church, where he looked for a kind of legitimate exile. Yet each time his exile took shape, his restless wandering would begin anew.[8]

Bonhoeffer's cultural exile culminated in his decision to join the plot to assassinate Hitler. As Robert Coles notes,

To stand outside the gates of money and power and rank and approved success and applause, to be regarded as irregular or odd or "sick" or, that final exile, as a traitor—such an outcome, in this era, carries its own special burdens and demands: the disapproval, if not derision, of colleagues, neighbors, the larger world of commentators who meticulously fall in line with reigning authority, but perhaps most devastating of all, the sense of oneself that is left in one's mind at the end of a day. What *am* I trying to do—and is this, after all, not only futile, but evidence that I have gone astray? In that regard, those of us who have been granted the right to decide what is "normal" or "abnormal" ought to be nervous, indeed, by the likes of a . . . Bonhoeffer.[9]

Finally, Bonhoeffer's theology is filled with the urgent zeal of the biblical prophets, such as Jeremiah announcing the coming destruction of Jerusalem and the exile that was sure to follow. Bonhoeffer frequently quotes the short but powerful Jeremiah 45 in his letters. He speaks of his own time as one in which people must live *etsi Deus non daretur*, or even if there were no God. He writes, "And we cannot be honest unless we recognize that we have to live in the world *etsi Deus non daretur*. . . . God would have us know that we must live as men who manage our lives without him. . . . God lets himself be pushed out of the world on to the cross."[10] In other words, we live in exile from God, or, more provocatively stated, God is exiled from the world. Bonhoeffer's letters are filled with intriguing thoughts such as these. We will concentrate on three of them.

Bonhoeffer's *Letters and Papers from Prison*

The category of exile serves as the organizing principle for our investigation of Bonhoeffer's letters. Exile involves a loss of a former way of life, a present state of uncertainty, and a proposed course of action for the future. The loss is summarized best by Bonhoeffer's comment that "Jesus calls men, not to a new religion, but to life."[11] The state of uncertainty following the loss of religion is described by Bonhoeffer as "the world come of age." He writes, "The question is: Christ and the world that has come of age."[12] Finally, for the future, Bonhoeffer makes the following clarion call: "Man is summoned to share in God's sufferings at the hands of a godless world."[13]

In these three thought-provoking sentences, we find some of the most enduring concepts in Bonhoeffer's theological legacy. We turn now to a closer examination of each of them.

"Jesus calls men, not to a new religion, but to life."

Bonhoeffer contends that the age of religion has ceased to exist. He does not, however, mourn its passing. Clifford Green explains, "In Bonhoeffer's judgment, religion has been a garment that Christianity has worn in various modes throughout its history; and while this garment may have been warm, comfortable, flattering to the wearer, and even according to the finest pattern of its type, it must now be discarded."[14]

What, then, did Bonhoeffer mean by *religion?* Larry L. Rasmussen offers the following summary:

To characterize religion he uses pejoratively such terms as *deus ex machina* (the God-of-the-gaps); provinciality (religion as a separated sector of one's life); metaphysics (thinking in two realms, the supernatural completing the natural); individual inwardness (pietism or other forms of ascetic escape); indispensability (a religious a priori as constitutive of human nature); and sanction (religion as the protector of privilege).[15]

While Bonhoeffer does not treat this topic in any systematic fashion, he does seem to propose two arguments in his letters: the first is historical, and the second is theological. Bonhoeffer reads the history of Christianity, politics, and science as a movement away from religion. He insists that an honest reading of the intellectual tradition of the West will lead the reasonable person to acknowledge the cultural fact that "God as a working hypothesis in morals, politics, or science, has been surmounted and abolished; and the same thing has happened in philosophy and religion (Feuerbach!)."[16]

The loss of religion is a welcome development for Bonhoeffer, therefore, because it signals a new awareness of God. Kelly notes that Bonhoeffer "opposed all efforts to make God the postulated answer to human weakness, a *deus ex machina* hovering over the stage of life, ready to descend to the rescue. God becomes thus only a 'working hypothesis' foisted on people as substitute for their own autonomy in and responsibility to the world."[17] The understanding of God as the One who calls us to turn our gaze from this world, to seek our own personal salvation, and to focus on our own personal weaknesses is replaced with an understanding of God as the One who turns our eye to our neighbor, to concern ourselves with the welfare of others, and to share in the suffering of God in this world. This is, for Bonhoeffer, an affirmation of the painful process of Christian maturation. The loss of religion is a transition from an earlier, more confident, yet magical understanding of God's activity in the world to an admittedly more awkward, yet ultimately more responsible understanding of God by the "world come of age."

"The question is: Christ and the world that has come of age."

The second of Bonhoeffer's thought-provoking ideas is "Christ and the world that has come of age." Rasmussen offers the following explanation:

> Bonhoeffer designates the increase of human autonomy by various forms of the German "*muendig*." The person who is "*muendig*" is one who "speaks for himself." The reference is to the passage from adolescence to adulthood. One is no longer a minor but is on his own. He has "come of age." He is now fully responsible for his actions. The reader of Bonhoeffer in English should note carefully that "*muendig*" is thus a reference to moral *accountability* and not moral maturity. That is, Bonhoeffer is saying that man is fully responsible for his actions whether he acts childishly, immaturely, irresponsibly, or whatever. The world's adulthood is in part, then, Bonhoeffer's designation of man's irrevocable responsibility for his answers to life's questions, together with all the consequences. Man can no longer return to an adolescent dependence upon a father to whom final responsibility falls.[18]

Bonhoeffer correlates his understanding of Jesus with "the world come of age." The loss of religion signals the close of one era in Christian history; "the world come of age" signals the transition into a new era, one that Bonhoeffer suggests may actually be in greater accordance with the gospel than the religion preached throughout most of Christian history.

Historically, religion has offered God as a source of comfort for people experiencing doubt and trouble and as a source of assurance for people confronting the painful riddle of death. Bonhoeffer regards the continued attempt to speak of God in this way as a misguided endeavor. Such an effort rests on certain assumptions about God and the world that "the world come of age" will no longer accept. Bonhoeffer insists that "man has learnt to deal with himself in all questions of importance without recourse to the 'working hypothesis' called 'God.'"[19] People do not expect God to act unilaterally to bring about a desired state of affairs here on Earth. The failure of much of modern Christian theology lies in its attempt to convince the world that it needs the God of religion. Bonhoeffer argues that this approach removes God from the center of people's day-to-day existence and characterizes God only in terms of "boundary situations" or "ultimate questions" of life. As William Kuhns explains,

> The man come of age is one whose work, family, education, and awareness of the world have made daily recourse to God unnecessary. He attempts no conscious movement of atheism and would not admit he was an atheist; very possibly he attends church on Sunday mornings. Yet he does not think that he needs God; and the preaching he hears, the books he may read, the sin he is told surrounds him—these do not summon the whole man, in complete involvement, as do his family, his work, his friendships. In short, he is a man able to live a human relatively complete life in the midst of a secular culture and with an immense confidence in that culture—without God.[20]

This failure on the part of many modern Christians to grasp the new situation presented by the world come of age compounds itself by proposing an outmoded view of Christ. What, then, is the proper understanding of Jesus in the world come of age?

Bonhoeffer's answer to that crucial question is that "Christ takes hold of man at the centre of his life"[21] and that Jesus is "the man for others."[22] Christ does not call us away from the world but rather into the world. Christ participates in the world, and Christians participate in Christ. We participate not only in Christ's ultimate victory but also in Christ's suffering. Christians, in other words, spiritually keep watch with Christ in the Garden of Gethsemane.

"Man is summoned to share in God's sufferings at the hands of a godless world."

Like Jesus in the Garden of Gethsemane, Christians are called to partake in the suffering of God. William Hamilton explains, "God may have withdrawn from the world, but he has not withdrawn from us. As Bonhoeffer had said earlier, and which we are now prepared to understand, 'God allows himself to be edged out of the world and on to the cross.' (16 July 1944). The world come of age is now seen as the world in which God suffers."[23]

In this letter of July 16, 1944, Bonhoeffer sees participation in God's suffering as the most appropriate understanding of the divine-human relationship in a world come of age—an understanding that is, in Bonhoeffer's eyes, closer to the one proclaimed by Jesus than the one preached in churches for most of Christian history. According to Bonhoeffer, "Only the suffering God can help."[24] In a letter written two days later, Bonhoeffer continues his discussion of this theme: "Jesus asked in Gethsemane, 'Could you not watch with me one hour?' That is a reversal of what the religious man expects from God. Man is summoned to share in God's sufferings at the hands of a godless world. . . . It is not the religious act that makes the Christian, but participation in the suffering of God in the secular life."[25] The Christian is called to suffer with God in Christ, to put Christ at the center of his or her life, and to affirm the world, not flee from it.

Assessments of Bonhoeffer's *Letters* and *Papers from Prison*

Bonhoeffer's letters from prison have yielded widely varying interpretations. This is due, in large part, to the nature of the writings themselves. They were not theological treatises intended for public scrutiny. As Charles Marsh notes, "Bonhoeffer's final book, *The Letters and Papers from Prison*, illustrates not only textual but theological fragmentariness as well. Yet the power of the book lies precisely in its 'trial combinations' and 'lightning flashes' of theological insight."[26] The bulk of the letters are written to Bonhoeffer's faithful friend, Eberhard Bethge, who served as his sounding board for his theological musings.

It is also important to remember that Bonhoeffer composed these letters while facing an uncertain future and suffering the constant monotony and frustration of more than a year's time in prison. In addition to the burden of confinement, Bonhoeffer experienced air raids, medical problems, and the despondency of some of his fellow prisoners. Of course, we will never know what a mature Bonhoeffer, living in postwar Germany, would have made of the various theological thoughts that he recorded in his prison correspondence.

Because *Letters and Papers from Prison* is not a sustained, book-length argument, readers have not so much offered various *criticisms* of the work as much as various *interpretations*. The theologian Thomas Torrance once complained that many interpreters of Bonhoeffer

have come to use Bonhoeffer for their own ends, as a means of objectifying their own image of themselves. . . . In this way, Bonhoeffer's thought has been severely twisted and misunderstanding of him has become rife, especially when certain catch-phrases like "religionless Christianity" and "worldly holiness" are worked up into systems of thought so sharply opposed to Bonhoeffer's basic Christian theology, not least his Christology.[27]

Some thinkers have interpreted Bonhoeffer as a prophet for an era in which formal religion will no longer address the needs of people, while others have seen in his work a radical focus on the Christ found in the gospels, rather than the often domesticated version of Christ proclaimed in the churches. As we read these letters decades after Bonhoeffer's death, we can only speculate about the direction in which his thought was headed.

Bonhoeffer's Spirituality

We proceed first with a brief examination of Bonhoeffer's own personal spirituality and second with the spiritual vision developed in a fragmentary way in the prison letters.

We get hints of Bonhoeffer's spirituality early in his career when he served as director of the underground seminary and later in the scattered references to his own devotional practices that are contained in his prison letters. Kelly notes,

> In a Germany geared for war, Bonhoeffer's seminary was described as an oasis of peace and spiritual freedom. The community began each morning with prayer and meditation. Their life together included daily prayers, personal confession, Bonhoeffer's own lectures, and discussions on preaching and the spiritual life.
>
> It was a regimen considered by some of the seminarians as a bit strict.[28]

James W. Woelfel offers the following account of Bonhoeffer's devotional practices while in prison:

> Bonhoeffer's own life of prayer, meditation, liturgical observance, and pastoral work while in prison is the

most impressive testimony of all to the "secret discipline" which is the inner foundation and sustenance of "religionless Christianity." . . .

He experienced "arid" periods which he mentioned quite frankly, when he was unable to make himself read the Bible, but daily reading and meditation following the *Losungen* was at the heart of his spiritual discipline. In the letter which initiated his remarks on "religionless Christianity," Bonhoeffer mentions his practice of reading the Bible "every morning and evening." There can be no doubt that his continued practice of grounding his daily life in the Word of God was an incalculable source of strength to him throughout his imprisonment.[29]

Bonhoeffer's letters are filled with references to scriptural passages and German hymns. Kelly comments that "prayer in solitude and fellowship in God's Word were, in fact, the very soul of Bonhoeffer's spirituality. This was the sustenance which carried him through the years of crisis and imprisonment."[30]

We turn now to the spiritual sustenance Bonhoeffer offers to the "world come of age." He makes an interesting suggestion: "The world that has come of age is more godless, and perhaps for that very reason nearer to God, than the world before its coming of age."[31] What, then, does the world come of age realize that draws it closer to God? The answer may be found in a line from a letter Bonhoeffer wrote to his fiancée: "Our marriage shall be a yes to God's earth; it shall strengthen our courage to act and accomplish something on earth. I fear that Christians who stand with only one leg upon earth also stand with only one leg in heaven."[32] Religion is individualistic and focused on the afterlife. By contrast, the Christian life in the world come of age is "a silent and hidden affair"[33] of human solidarity and worldly involvement. The world come of age realizes, to borrow one of Bonhoeffer's more cryptic sayings, that "God is beyond in the midst of our life."[34]

The Future of Secular Theology

Admirers of *Letters and Papers from Prison* have enlisted Bonhoeffer as a spokesperson for their various causes, but his greatest influence was on the *secular theology* movement of the 1960s and 1970s. While the label *secular theology* served as an umbrella term for a variety of theological positions, Harvey Cox was often identified as one of its leading proponents. In his work *Secular City,* Cox argued that secularization presented a challenge to traditional Christianity that theologians had not adequately addressed.[35] *Secularization* refers to the social process in which religious understandings of the world and humans' place in it lose their dominance. Members of a secularized culture do not interpret all events in their lives in religious terms. Many secular theologians regarded Bonhoeffer's *Letters and Papers from Prison* as a prophetic work that accurately described the world in which they now lived.

One of the most lasting contributions of secular theology to Christian thought is the reminder that theology arises from and speaks to a particular context. First, theologians themselves are working in particular cultural, social, and religious contexts. What questions are they asking? What assumptions are they making? What solutions are they proposing? Second, we as readers are also bringing to the theological work our own sets of concerns, interests, and assumptions. Each of us might ask, Does this theology speak to my own personal situation? Is this theology meaningful to the church I attend? Are the solutions being proposed desirable to me? Questions such as these may also help us understand why certain theological works connect with one group of readers but not others. Third, the issue of context plays a prominent role in missionary efforts. How can a religious tradition that is Western in its language, style of worship, and outlook be faithfully expressed in a significantly different culture? What alternate forms of worship, for example, would be acceptable? Which customs in the culture can be integrated into the faith practices of the church? Which customs are incompatible with Christian faith?

As we move ahead in the twenty-first century of Christian thought, secular theologians force us to assess the world in which we live. Is it accurate to describe our culture as *secular*? Is God irrelevant for most people in terms of how they understand their lives? If so, how can theologians craft positions that best address this situation? In responding to these questions, we can consider many of the lines that Bonhoeffer penned in the Tegel Prison over fifty years ago.

Conclusion

Exilic prophets such as Ezekiel offered hope to Jewish exiles by proclaiming that God had not abandoned them and that they would once again worship God in a new temple in Jerusalem. In a similar vein, in a letter written on the occasion of the baptism of young Dietrich Bethge, Bonhoeffer holds out hope for the future:

> It is not for us to prophesy the day (though the day will come) when men will once more be called so to utter the word of God that the world will be changed and renewed by it. It will be a new language, perhaps quite non-religious, but liberating and redeeming—as was Jesus' language; it will shock people and yet overcome them by its power; it will be the language of a new righteousness and truth, proclaiming God's peace with men and the coming of his kingdom.[36]

When the Jews did return to the promised land, they incorporated much of what they had learned while in

Babylon into their theology. That type of theological synthesis will be the model for our next theologian, Sallie McFague.

◎ Discussion Questions

1. Which life experiences are forms of exile?
2. Was it proper for Bonhoeffer, a Christian pastor, to be involved in the plot to assassinate Adolf Hitler? Why or why not?
3. What is Bonhoeffer's understanding of religion? Do you agree or disagree with that understanding?
4. Do we as a culture no longer accept God as "a working hypothesis" when solving our problems? If so, is that a positive or negative development? Do we live in a "world come of age"?
5. Is Christ best thought of as "a man for others"? How does that understanding of Jesus relate to your own understanding of Jesus?
6. What does it mean "to share in God's sufferings"?
7. In your view, is Bonhoeffer's theology positive or negative?

◎ Notes

1. John Bright, *A History of Israel*, 3rd ed. (Philadelphia: Westminster Press, 1981), p. 343.

2. John G. Gager, *The Origins of Anti-Semitism* (New York: Oxford University Press, 1983), p. 13.

3. For biographical information on Bonhoeffer, I rely heavily on chapter 1 of Dallas Roark, *Dietrich Bonhoeffer* (Waco, Tex.: Word Books, 1972); chapter 1 of Geffrey B. Kelly, *Liberating Faith* (Minneapolis: Augsburg, 1984); and chapter 12 of William Kuhns, *In Pursuit of Dietrich Bonhoeffer* (Dayton, Ohio: Pfalaum Press, 1967).

4. Roark, *Dietrich Bonhoeffer*, p. 16.

5. Kelly, *Liberating Faith*, p. 28.

6. Quoted in Kelly, *Liberating Faith*, p. 27.

7. Franklin Sherman, "Dietrich Bonhoeffer," in Marty E. Marty and Dean G. Peerman, eds., *A Handbook of Christian Theologians* (Nashville, Tenn.: Abingdon Press, 1984), pp. 465–466.

8. Eberhard Bethge, *Bonhoeffer: Exile and Martyr* (New York: Seabury Press, 1975), p. 107.

9. Robert Coles, "The Making of a Disciple," in *Dietrich Bonhoeffer* (Maryknoll, N.Y.: Orbis Books, 1998), p. 40.

10. Dietrich Bonhoeffer, *Letters and Papers from Prison*, enlarged ed., edited by Eberhard Bethge (New York: Touchstone Books, 1971), p. 360.

11. Bonhoeffer, *Letters and Papers*, p. 362.

12. Ibid., p. 327.

13. Ibid., p. 361.

14. Clifford Green, "Bonhoeffer's Concept of Religion," *Union Seminary Quarterly Review* 19, no. 1 (1963): 11.

15. Larry L. Rasmussen, *Dietrich Bonhoeffer: Reality and Resistance* (Nashville, Tenn.: Abingdon Press, 1972), pp. 81–82.

16. Bonhoeffer, *Letters and Papers*, p. 360.

17. Kelly, *Liberating Faith*, p. 75.

18. Rasmussen, *Dietrich Bonhoeffer*, p. 81.

19. Bonhoeffer, *Letters and Papers*, p. 325.

20. William Kuhns, *In Pursuit of Dietrich Bonhoeffer* (Dayton, Ohio: Pflaum Press, 1967), p. 195.

21. Bonhoeffer, *Letters and Papers*, p. 337.

22. Ibid., p. 382.

23. William Hamilton, "'The Letters Are a Particular Thorn': Some Themes in Bonhoeffer's Prison Writings," in Roger Gregor Smith, ed., *World Come of Age* (London: Collins, 1967), p. 155.

24. Bonhoeffer, *Letters and Papers*, p. 361.

25. Ibid., p. 361.

26. Charles Marsh, "Dietrich Bonhoeffer," in David F. Ford, ed., *The Modern Theologians*, 2nd ed. (Oxford: Blackwell, 1997), p. 47.

27. Thomas Torrance, "Cheap and Costly Grace," *God and Rationality* (Oxford: Oxford University Press, 1971), p. 74. Quoted in Ralf K. Wustenberg, "Religionless Christianity: Dietrich Bonhoeffer's Tegel Theology," in John W. de Gruchy, *Bonhoeffer for a New Day* (Grand Rapids, Mich.: Eerdmans, 1997), p. 58.

28. Kelly, *Liberating Faith*, pp. 24–25.

29. James W. Woelfel, *Bonhoeffer's Theology: Classical and Revolutionary* (Nashville, Tenn.: Abingdon, 1970), pp. 200–201. Bethge informs us that the *Losungen* were "daily texts, published yearly since 1731" (*Letters and Papers*, p. 265). Bonhoeffer mentions the *Losungen* in the letter written on Christmas Eve, 1943.

30. Kelly, *Liberating Faith*, p. 144.

31. Bonhoeffer, *Letters and Papers*, p. 362.

32. Ibid., p. 415.

33. Ibid., p. 300.

34. Ibid., p. 282.

35. Harvey Cox, *The Secular City: Secularization and Urbanization in Theological Perspective*, 2nd ed. (New York: Macmillan, 1966) pp. 2–3.

36. Bonhoeffer, *Letters and Papers*, p. 300.

◉ Suggested Readings

For a study of the exile, see Peter R. Ackroyd, *Exile and Restoration* (Philadelphia: Westminster, 1968), and Ralph W. Klein, *Israel in Exile* (Philadelphia: Fortress, 1979).

For an anthology of Bonhoeffer's writings, see Geffrey B. Kelly and F. Burton Nelson, *A Testament to Freedom* (San Francisco: HarperSanFrancisco, 1995).

For a short introduction to Bonhoeffer's entire theology, see any of the following: Charles Marsh, "Dietrich Bonhoeffer," in David F. Ford, ed., *The Modern Theologians*, 2nd ed. (Oxford: Blackwell, 1997); Franklin Sherman, "Dietrich Bonhoeffer," in Martin E. Marty and Dean G. Peerman, eds., *A Handbook of Christian Theologians* (Nashville, Tenn.: Abingdon Press, 1984); and Stanley J. Grenz and Roger E. Olson, *Twentieth-Century Theology* (Downers Grove, Ill.: InterVarsity Press, 1992), pp. 146–156. See also *Christian History* Issue 32 X(4).

For book-length treatments, see Geffrey B. Kelly, *Liberating Faith* (Minneapolis: Augsburg, 1984); William Kuhn, *In Pursuit of Dietrich Bonhoeffer* (Dayton, Ohio: Pflaum Press, 1967); John D. Godsey, *The Theology of Dietrich Bonhoeffer* (Philadelphia: Westminster Press, 1960); Dallas Roark, *Dietrich Bonhoeffer* (Waco, Tex.: Word Books, 1972); and John W. de Grunchy, ed., *The Cambridge Companion to Dietrich Bonhoeffer* (Cambridge: Cambridge University Press, 1999). Chapter 12 of the *Cambridge Companion to Dietrich Bonhoeffer*, "Christianity in a World Come of Age," by Peter Selby, is also a very helpful resource. For an interesting discussion of Bonhoeffer, see chapters 1 and 2 of Stanley Hauerwas, *Performing the Faith* (Grand Rapids, Mich.: Brazos Press, 2004).

Chapter 5

Restoration: Sallie McFague and Liberal Theology

What can Christians learn from the wider culture?

> ✤ *Looking Ahead*
>
> Sallie McFague (1933–) is a Christian theologian whose work represents the long tradition of liberal theology. It focuses on ecological and political crises and how God interacts with human beings in the natural world to help us ensure our survival. Pay attention to how McFague understands her work as an exercise in 'metaphorical theology,' which takes seriously how descriptions of God, humans, and nature affect how we conceive of God, and questions how we are challenged to live as Christians.

The painful separation from the promised land, the grief caused by the destruction of the temple, and the anguish of being exiled in a pagan culture did not stop the Jews from either practicing their faith or thinking in new and creative ways about God's relationship with the world. In fact, Scripture scholars have long held that one of the sources for the book of Genesis took shape during the Babylonian exile. One of the passages that most clearly reflects the influence of Babylonian thought on the Bible is the first creation story (1:1—2:4). These opening chapters of the Bible reflect an engagement with the Babylonian creation story known as the *Enuma Elish*, and they also provide a helpful analogy of the modern theological movement known as *liberalism*.

When the Jews were in Babylon, they would have encountered the ancient *Enuma Elish*, in which creation occurs after the gods Tiamat and Marduk battle and Marduk, the victor, creates the heavens and the earth from the slain body of Tiamat. The chronology of events in the *Enuma Elish*—involving the creation of light, the sky, the land, the stars, and so on—may have influenced the biblical writers in their crafting of the first story of creation. In general terms, the Jews accepted some features of the Babylonian creation story but rejected its core theology. As the Jews became familiar with Babylonian thought, they absorbed some of its beliefs and rejected others. This pattern would be repeated throughout Jewish and Christian history.

The ethicist James Gustafson offers three options that religious believers have in addressing claims of truth from nontheological sources: (1) reject the claim, (2) absorb the claim and allow it to determine your theology, or (3) make some theological accommodation with the claim.[1] Gustafson advocates the third approach as a general policy, and this is the approach typically designated as *liberalism*. This is not to suggest that all theories or beliefs should be accommodated but rather that theologians are open to reformulating their positions in light of developments in other areas of inquiry.[2] Historically, we can see how Christians reassessed their interpretation of Genesis in light of the theory of evolution and abandoned their endorsement of slavery in light of Enlightenment claims about universal human rights.

For the contemporary theologian Sallie McFague, Christian theology needs to rethink its central claims in light of the global threats of ecological and nuclear devastation or possible annihilation and the broad political and social culture in which such threats are managed.

That is precisely the task she undertakes in her work *Models of God*.

Biography of Sallie McFague

Models of God grew out of McFague's own theological journey. In a later work, she would recount the four "conversions" she experienced that significantly altered her thinking. The first of these occurred when she was a young girl and realized her own mortality. She writes, "One day while walking home from school the thought came to me that some day I would not be here; I would not exist. Christmas would come, and I would not be around to celebrate it; even more shocking, my birthday would occur, and I would not be present."[3] This experience also prompted the opposite realization: a greater awareness that all reality had its origin and continued existence in God.

McFague's second conversion came in college while she was reading Karl Barth's *Commentary on Romans*. With its uncompromising insistence on God's transcendence, Barth's bombshell work opened up for McFague an entirely new way of thinking about God. "My boxed-in, comfortable, tribal notion of God was split wide open and like a cold, bracing mountain wind, the awesome presence of the divine brushed my life."[4] McFague's enchantment with Barth's theology began to wane as she came to sense the presence of God through nature, a position at odds with Barth's insistence that God's revelation is found exclusively in Christ. She writes, "Nature can seduce us with its beauty and right order to love and glorify God. This is what happened to me."[5]

McFague's ecological sensibilities laid the foundation for her third conversion. While teaching at Vanderbilt Divinity School, she was deeply impressed by the contention of the theologian Gordon Kaufman that, in McFague's words, "given the nuclear and ecological crises facing our planet, theology could no longer proceed with business as usual. It must deconstruct and reconstruct its central symbols—God, Christ, human being—from within this new context."[6] This is essentially the project of *Models of God*, which we will explore.

McFague's fourth conversion involves a deeper turn to the spiritual life and what the seventeenth-century Brother Lawrence famously called "the practice of the presence of God." McFague writes, "Finally, after years of talking *about* God (what theologians are paid to do!), I am becoming acquainted *with* God."[7]

McFague's *Models of God*

Models of God is an exercise in *metaphorical theology*. In the first part, McFague outlines the key features of a metaphorical theology, and in the second part, she engages in the actual practice of metaphorical theology by offering three models of God that she argues are relevant for our day and age: God as mother, lover, and friend.

What, then, is *metaphorical theology*? The most comprehensive description focuses on the use and misuse of religious language. The religious language that we employ (especially the images we use) in preaching, teaching, and liturgy conveys a certain understanding of the Christian life. Metaphorical theology is highly conscious of the suggestive power of religious language. For instance, picturing the world being ruled by a benevolent king as opposed to being nurtured by a loving mother results in distinctly different understanding of God's relation to the world and humans' place within it.

Metaphorical theology has, by its own admission, a "tentative, relative, partial, and hypothetical character."[8] The metaphors that dominated the religious imaginations of Christians generations ago may no longer be appropriate for our time, and the images of today may not respond to the deepest religious questions of future generations. Metaphors, as well as analogies and parables, tease the mind into considering how, for example, war is like and unlike a game of chess.[9] In this context, McFague offers one of her most controversial observations about metaphorical theology: "What this sort of enterprise makes very clear is that theology is *mostly* fiction: it is the elaboration of key metaphors and models."[10]

McFague's metaphorical theology puts great emphasis on the need for theology to be meaningful for our time. But what about its rootedness in the past, especially in the biblical writings and the classic theological works in the Christian tradition? For McFague, Scripture and tradition "both are witnesses to the experiences of the salvific power of God."[11] What is theologically decisive for McFague is the experience to which both Scripture and tradition testify. "Scripture and the classics of the theological tradition, are 'sedimentations' of interpreted experience."[12] The practical consequence that follows is that Scripture provides, in McFague's view, "a model of how theology should be done, rather than as the authority dictating the terms in which it is done."[13]

Critics would obviously charge that McFague's proposal does not give sufficient weight to the authority of Scripture. Contrary to what McFague argues, her critics would contend that Scripture does indeed have the authority to dictate the terms of a Christian theology. Without such a restriction, they would insist, theological positions could be generated at the whim of the theologian. McFague would counter her critics by insisting that there is a core belief to the Christian account: "To believe in the God of the Judeo-Christian tradition is to believe in the trustworthiness of things or that the power in the universe is gracious."[14]

Because the Christian message finds its specificity in the life, death, and resurrection of Jesus Christ, McFague asks, "Are there distinguishable marks of the story of Jesus that are relevant to a holistic, nuclear age?" McFague identifies three aspects of Jesus' ministry that give rise to the "destabilizing, inclusive, nonhierarchical vision for all of creation" that is at the heart of the Christian message.[15] McFague highlights Jesus' parables, his table fellowship with outcasts, and his crucifixion as three features of the gospel that are valuable resources for contemporary theology.

The power of the parables lies in their ability to subvert our expectations about the kingdom of God. Nowhere is this better illustrated than in the parable of the good Samaritan (Luke 10:30-37). The despised Samaritan is praised as the one who does the will of God, while the priest and Levite do not respond to their neighbor (possibly because contact with the bloodied victim would violate purity laws). As McFague notes, the parables challenge the cultural distinction between the worthy and unworthy. She recommends that we apply that type of reasoning to our own world, challenge our common distinction between human and nonhuman reality, and come to value the entire cosmos.

The second valuable resource McFague identifies is Jesus' table fellowship with outcasts. Jesus' willingness to eat with tax collectors and sinners violated the social and religious conventions of his day but demonstrated the inclusive nature of the kingdom of God. McFague again extends that vision in our own situation to include the nonhuman world, as well.

Third, the cross stands as the world's response to those who challenge the current social and political order with the radical vision of God's kingdom. The cross is the symbolic fate of all who challenge the powers that be. For McFague, the appearance stories of the risen Christ assure us of "the promise of God to be permanently present, 'bodily' present to us, in all places and times of our world."[16] From this idea, McFague proposes that we think metaphorically of the universe as God's body, as opposed to what she labels "the monarchical model" of the God-world relationship.

The traditional language of God as King suggests that all power rests with the monarch and that, as faithful subjects, we should surrender our will to that of the King. McFague sees three flaws with this model: "God is distant from the world, relates only to the human world, and controls that world through domination and benevolence."[17] She believes that royal language suggests that God's kingdom is an otherworldly reality, far removed from the mundane workings of our world. Moreover, because plants cannot hear and obey, the King's loyal subjects are almost always understood to be human beings. This relegates the nonhuman world to a secondary status in the eyes of God. It also generates a sense of passivity on the part of humans. Because all power resides with God, humans seem exempt from responsibility to care for the world. Seeing the world as God's body, insists McFague, addresses these deficiencies. God knows the world in a way that is similar to the way we know our own joys and pains. Just as we are concerned about our own health, God is concerned about the well-being of the world. God wants all humans to have adequate food and shelter, and God suffers when the planet is poisoned.

After McFague states the need for new and imaginative ways of picturing the relationship between God and the world, she devotes herself to just that task in the second part of her book, where she proposes the metaphors of God as mother, lover, and friend. Not only are all three metaphors suggestive of intimacy and relatedness, but they also correspond to the three Greek words that translate as "love." The word *agape* is a love concerned with the other, and the Greeks used this word to describe the love of a parent for a child. *Eros* is the love characterized by desire; the Greeks spoke of romantic love as *eros*. The Greeks also wisely recognized the value of the friendship and reserved a unique designation, *philia*, for that form of love. To guard against an overly individualistic understanding of these three metaphors, McFague reminds us, "The Gospel of John gives the clue: for God so loved the *world*. It is not individuals who are loved by God as mother, lover, and friend but the world."[18]

To draw out the implications of these metaphors or models, McFague asks three questions about each of them: "What sort of divine love is suggested by each model? What kind of divine activity is implied by this love? What does each kind of love say about existence in our world?"[19] In short, these are the answers she offers. In the model of God as parent, the *agape* of God acts by creating us and calls us to foster justice. In the model of God as lover, the *eros* of God acts by saving us and calls us to foster healing. In the model of God as friend, the *philia* of God acts by sustaining us and calls us to foster companionship. In the course of her explication, McFague also offers her own reinterpretation of many of the traditional beliefs regarding God, Christ, the church, and so on. We will assess a select number of McFague's positions as we proceed through the second part of *Models of God*.

McFague argues that the model of God as mother allows us to think in different terms about the creation of the world. The traditional creation account emphasizes that God created the universe *ex nihilo*, or "out of nothing," and pictures a hierarchical arrangement to creation, beginning with God and descending to angels, to humans, and finally to inanimate objects. "Both of these notions," writes McFague, "support dualism: the absolute distinction of God from the world, and the inferiority of matter to spirit, body to mind."[20] The model of God as mother encourages us to think of creation as analogous to birth: "the universe is bodied forth from God."[21] McFague reminds us of the limitations of all models of God but argues that this model minimizes the difference and distance between God and the world and therefore provides a more holistic account of the relationship among God, humans, and the natural world.

The model of God as mother also recasts the traditional Christian conception of justice. Rather than view God's justice in terms of punishment to hell, "God as mother-judge is the one who establishes justice, not the one who hands out sentences. She is concerned with establishing justice now, not with condemning in the future."[22] The justice that McFague envisions is one of care for the entire creation that calls for a "universalizing of our most basic loves."[23] Just as a mother expresses her love for her children by nurturing them and allowing them to develop as individuals, God's love extends in similar way to all creation. Justice, then, is concerned with the conditions that allow all life to flourish in this world.

While Christians commonly speak of God loving humanity, rarely do they say that God is a lover. This second model of God that McFague proposes retrieves the language of desire found in mystical writers such as the twelfth-century monk Bernard of Clairvaux. The most compelling reason for viewing God's relationship with the world in terms of the human experience of *eros* is, according to McFague, that it speaks powerfully to the value of the one who is loved. The passionate love of God for the world, then, affirms the value of all creation. God's passionate concern for the well-being of all creation must, according to McFague, be reflected in our own response to the natural world.

It is also in the model of God as lover that McFague deals most directly with the theological topics of *christology* (the identity of Christ) and *soteriology* (the work of Christ). She writes, "Jesus' response as beloved to God as lover was so open and thorough that his life and death were revelatory of God's great love for the world."[24] Christ incarnates the love of God for the world. In terms of salvation, the traditional Christian understanding of this concept focuses on the death and resurrection of Christ. Christians have employed various images and metaphors (such as sacrifice, atonement, redemption) to describe how Christ's death and resurrection brought about salvation and victory over the power of sin and death. Despite the diversity of expression, there is a unanimity in their understanding that Christ alone is the savior of the world. He won the victory *for* us but not *with* us.

For McFague, Jesus is the "premier paradigm of God's love" or the exemplar of God's love for the world for Christians. "His illumination of that love as inclusive of the last and the least, as embracing and valuing the outcast, is paradigmatic of God the lover but is not unique."[25] Likewise, the work of salvation is not uniquely Christ's. "Salvation is not a once-for-all objective service that someone else does for us. Rather, it is the ongoing healing of the divided body of our world which we, with God, work at together."[26] McFague insists that "there must be many saviors."[27]

The third of McFague's models views the God-world relationship through the lens of the friendships that sustain us over the course of our lives. "God as sustainer—as the very word suggests—is the One who endures, who bears the weight of the world, working for its fulfillment, rejoicing and suffering with it, permanently."[28] The model of God as friend does not work in isolation from the previous models of God as mother and lover bur rather expands on the earlier insights. The God who creates and saves us also sustains us. The God who calls us to be agents of justice and healing also calls us to companionship with God, neighbor, and the natural world. The trinitarian God whom Christians traditionally proclaim to be Father, Son, and Spirit is also Creator, Savior, and Sustainer.

The church is understood to be a community of friends who support each other through their joys and struggles. Joined by their common belief and purpose, these friends replicate the table fellowship that Jesus enacted in his ministry. The church community is therefore inclusive, offering hospitality to the stranger. The church is a group gathered for the breaking of the bread, both in its eucharistic meaning but also in its material meaning of providing basic needs to the poor. Finally, the church is a community of prayer who calls on "God the friend to support, forgive, and comfort us as we struggle together to save our beleaguered planet, our beautiful earth, our blue and green marble in a universe of silent rock and fire."[29]

Assessments of McFague's *Models of God*

We will focus on three areas in which McFague's critics have raised concerns about her arguments in *Models of God*. The first set of criticisms is methodological and addresses how McFague constructs a theological position and which sources she accords the most authority. The second set of criticisms concerns her orthodoxy. Does she advance positions that are at odds with the Christian faith? The third group of criticisms is philosophical and linguistic in character. What types of truth claims are being made with the use of metaphors?

Some of McFague's critics take issue with her theological method—specifically, with her claim that Scripture provides "a model of how theology should be done," rather than "the authority dictating the terms in which it is done."[30] For McFague, Scripture is the expression of the experiences of the early church communities and reflects the diverse traditions within the early church. She does not maintain, however, that the content of the canonical writings is normative for contemporary Christian theological thought. Her critics ask, Does this position safeguard the essential beliefs of the Christian faith, as found in Scripture? The theologian Warren McWilliams writes,

> McFague's view of the authority of the Bible in relation to her choice of models for God will raise questions for some, especially evangelical theologians. She seems to

have elevated experience over the objective authority of the Bible. . . . She may be right that it is artificial to try to separate scripture, experience, and tradition, but evangelical theologians generally would insist on a higher level of authority for the Bible than she seems to give it.[31]

Furthermore, does McFague's view undermine her own appeals to Jesus' ministry (parables, table fellowship, crucifixion) as expressing a view of the world that we should adopt? McFague contends that "the theologian is constrained to return to the paradigmatic story of Jesus for validation and illumination."[32] McFague validates her own proposals by referencing elements of Jesus' ministry, but if Scripture has no binding force, then what has been achieved by such validation?

The second set of criticisms follows from the first. Some critics charge that because McFague does not give sufficient weight to the content of Scripture, some of her reinterpretations of traditional Christian beliefs go astray. In his review of *Models of God*, Roderick T. Leupp writes,

The book will provoke the timid and the scrupulously orthodox. There is much to turn the head and grind the teeth. The writer of Psalm 51 anguished that he had sinned solely against God, but not so McFague. Sin is against nature and other people, God's presence therein implied. It is true that John Wesley proclaimed that "there is no holiness but social holiness," but even so he kept firmly in sight the "over against" quality of God. This "absolute qualitative difference between God and man" has vanished for McFague. The dissipation extends to Jesus, who is "not ontologically different from other paradigmatic figures either in our tradition or in other religious traditions."[33]

Leupp expresses concern about McFague's understanding of sin and Christ. However, other problems would include her contention that "in some sense God is physical,"[34] or her claim "that God needs the world,"[35] or her suggestion that "God is involved in evil."[36]

The third set of criticisms centers on McFague's discussion of metaphors. She positions a metaphorical theology between the two extremes of *fundamentalism* and *deconstructionism*. In her estimation, the fundamentalists err by attaching a literal meaning to an image (for instance, God as Father) that is meant to be symbolic, and the deconstructionists err by insisting that language does not refer to anything in reality. McFague reminds us that a metaphor functions by comparing two things, prompting the listener to see how the two are like and unlike. For example, the Lord is like a shepherd in terms of guidance and protection but unlike a shepherd in terms of not being a human being. On the one hand, the fundamentalists fail to recognize how the two elements in a metaphor are unlike each other. To call God "Father" does not mean that God is a male deity but simply that God is, in some sense, like a father. On the other hand, deconstructionists fail to see how the elements of a metaphor are alike. They insist that there is no connection between God and "Father."

Critics, however, argue that, in her own position, McFague gives greater weight to the deconstructionists' view. "The essence of metaphorical theology, . . ." she insists, "is precisely the refusal to identify human constructions with divine reality."[37] Because there "is no way behind our constructions to test them for their correspondence with the reality they presume to represent," the best we can do is judge the metaphors by the way of life that they generate if they are accepted.[38] In an evaluation of McFague's theology, the theologian Byron C. Bangert believes that "what is lacking is precisely the 'sense of reality' that she claims is necessary for an account of the God-world relationship to be credible and persuasive. A truly compelling theological construal needs to be able to claim a greater congruity between theological metaphors and their referents, including both God and the world as it really is, or even as it possibly could be."[39]

It is in this context that Rosemary Radford Ruether presents her criticism of McFague's work:

> It is at this point that one must ask liberal relativists to come clean. Is this dominating God-language simply outworn, a language that was once right, but is so no longer? Or, was it, in fact, always wrong? McFague, like most liberal relativists, seems to straddle the fence. One aspect of her critique suggests that patriarchal God-talk is one metaphor among others, fine for its time, but no longer appropriate. Another side of her critique constantly exposes the evil ethical consequences of a God-language of domination that generates relationships of violence, illusionary separation, and impoverishing servility. If this is what this language does now, didn't it always do it?[40]

Ruether's position assumes that there is what Bangert called a "congruity between theological metaphors and their referents."[41] Inaccurate portraits of God are inaccurate in all times and in all places. The other approach is to measure a metaphor by what type of life it produces. In one century, calling God "King" might support a mission to help the poor, while in another century, the same language might result in the domination of a native culture. This technical philosophical and linguistic question has important implications for theological discussions about God.

The Future of Liberal Theology

The theologian Paul Tillich once identified a delicate balance that needs to be maintained in Christian theology between "the Protestant principle" and "Catholic substance."[42] By the former, he meant that no human institution or concept should be accorded divine status. By the latter, he meant that Christianity has no ultimate value if it is purely a human construct with no genuine contact with the divine.

McFague and other liberals skillfully bring the Protestant principle to bear on their work. They freely revise the elements of the received Christian tradition that they believe further our disregard for the welfare of the planet. Critics, however, insist that this impulse needs to be counterbalanced with a strong sense of the Catholic substance—that is, the belief that God's will has been revealed in some form in the actual life of the Christian community. Without this balance, Christian beliefs become purely human creations that can be molded at will. The danger, then, is that liberals advance their political, social, and economic ideas under the guise of Christian belief, rather than critically evaluate their political, social, and economic beliefs on the basis of the Christian message. The future of liberal theology depends on how well it can address this concern.

Conclusion

The Babylonian exile presented the Israelites with the external challenge of a competing creation story and also prompted an internal questioning of their own beliefs about their covenant with God. The restoration to the land presented a new set of concerns for the Israelites, from questions of Jewish identity to the practical matter of rebuilding the walls around Jerusalem.

As we have seen, the situation to which the theologian speaks is constantly changing. In this chapter, we have examined the proposals of Sallie McFague for a theology that is relevant to the twenty-first century. Her work is part of the liberal tradition that is open to readjusting the language and beliefs of the Christian tradition so the core message of the gospel can be heard anew by each generation. Our next thinker, the Roman Catholic theologian Karl Rahner, combines this liberal commitment to theological reconstruction with a traditional Catholic regard for the thought of the thirteenth-century theologian Thomas Aquinas.

⊚ Discussion Questions

1. What are some traditional Christian beliefs that have been altered in response to developments in fields outside theology?
2. What does McFague mean when she says that theology is "mostly fiction"? Do you agree or disagree with her?
3. What, if any, are the negative consequences of picturing God as King?
4. Is it helpful to think of the world as God's body? Why or why not?
5. What is your evaluation of McFague's proposed models of God as mother, lover, and friend?
6. Do biblical metaphors about God provide reliable information about the nature of God?
7. What is your overall evaluation of McFague's *Models of God?*

⊚ Notes

1. James M. Gustafson, *An Examined Faith* (Minneapolis: Fortress Press, 2004), pp. 6–7.
2. This raises a number of complex philosophical questions about truth and the justification of truth claims. Namely, when are we justified in believing that a certain proposition is true? For a helpful discussion of this complex topic, see Terrence Reynolds, "Two McFagues: Meaning, Truth, and Justification in *Models of God*," *Modern Theology* 11, no. 3 (1995): 289–313.
3. Sallie McFague, *Life Abundant* (Minneapolis: Fortress Press, 2001), p. 4.
4. McFague, *Life Abundant*, p. 5.
5. Ibid., p. 6.

6. Ibid., pp. 6–7.
7. Ibid., p. 8. Italics in original.
8. Sallie McFague, *Models of God* (Philadelphia: Fortress Press, 1987), p. 38.
9. McFague, *Models of God*, p. 33.
10. Ibid., pp. xi–xii. Italics in original.
11. Ibid., p. 42.
12. Ibid., p. 42.
13. Ibid., p. 43.
14. Ibid., p. 44
15. Ibid., p. 49.
16. Ibid., p. 60.
17. Ibid., p. 65.
18. Ibid., p. 86. Italics in original.
19. Ibid., p. 92.
20. Ibid., p. 109.
21. Ibid., p. 110.
22. Ibid., p. 118.
23. Ibid., p. 121.
24. Ibid., p. 136.
25. Ibid.
26. Ibid., p. 143.
27. Ibid., p. 150.
28. Ibid., p. 171.
29. Ibid., p. 180.
30. Ibid., p. 43.
31. Warren McWilliams, "God as Friend: A Test Case in Metaphorical Theology," *Perspectives in Religious Studies* 16, no. 2 (1989): 118.
32. McFague, *Models of God*, p. 49.
33. Roderick T. Leupp, review of Sallie McFague, *Models of God: Theology for an Ecological, Nuclear Age, Journal of the Evangelical Theological Society* 32, no. 2 (1989): 285.
34. McFague, *Models of God*, p. 112.
35. Ibid., p. 133.
36. Ibid., p. 75.
37. Ibid., p. 22.
38. Ibid., p. 26.
39. Byron C. Bangert, *Consenting to God and Nature* (Eugene, Ore.: Pickwick, 2006), pp. 143–144.

40. Rosemary Radford Ruether, "*Models of God*: Exploding the Foundations," *Religion and Intellectual Life* 5, no. 3 (1988): 22.

41. Bangert, *Consenting to God and Nature*, p. 143.

42. Paul Tillich, *Systematic Theology*, Volume Three (Chicago: University of Chicago Press, 1963), p. 245.

◎ Suggested Readings

For background on McFague's theology, see Gary Dorrien, *The Making of American Liberal Theology: Crisis, Irony, and Postmodernity 1950–2005* (Louisville, Ky.: Westminster John Knox Press, 2006), pp. 358–371. See also Ellen T. Armour, "Sallie McFague," in Donald W. Musser and Jospeh L. Price, eds., *A New Handbook of Christian Theologians* (Nashville, Tenn.: Abingdon, 1996), and chapter 3 of Byron C. Gangert, *Consenting to God and Nature* (Eugene, Ore.: Pickwick, 2006).

For reviews of *Models of God* from papers delivered at the American Academy of Religion, see *Religion and Intellectual Life* 3 (Spring 1988): 9–44. See also *Religious Studies Review* 16, no. 1 (1990): 36–42.

For McFague's contribution to *The Christian Century*'s "How My Mind Has Changed" series, see Sallie McFague, "An Earthly Theological Agenda," in *The Christian Century* 108, no. 1 (January 2–9, 1991): 12–15.

Chapter 6

Incarnation: Karl Rahner and Neo-Thomism

What is the meaning of Christ for twenty-first-century Christians?

✎*Looking Ahead*

Karl Rahner (1904–1984), whose work is described as Neo-Thomist, was arguably the leading Catholic theologian of the twentieth century. His theology takes as its foundation the work of Thomas Aquinas (thirteenth-century Catholic theologian and philosopher), whose systematic theology addresses questions about the whole of theology and attempts to unify the answers systematically in categorical structures. Note how Rahner, like other theologians, remains focused on the meaning of Christ for Christian living today.

In the opening chapter to *God Matters,* Graeme Garrett offers a interesting vantage point from which to survey the field of theology. He writes,

In his Gifford lectures of 1985 the Princeton physicist Freeman Dyson wrote: "God did not only create mountains, he also created jungles." Dyson was making a point about two types of science, two types of physics in fact. He called one the "unifying" and the other the "diversifying" type. Einstein and Maxwell are dominating examples of the first, the unifying type. Their concern is with "mountains." Throughout his life Einstein sought for a broad, rational, unified theory of the physical world and its components. His most famous shot at it was the theory of relativity. Maxwell plotted the dynamics of electromagnetism in a brief series of elegant, far-reaching equations. Both thinkers drew together vast ranges of experimental data in their theories. Their aim was to bring more and more of the observed phenomena within the scope of a few fundamental principles: in short, to discern the unity of things, how they hang together.

On the other hand, Rutherford and Eddington stand for Dyson's diversifying science. The diversifiers are in love with complexity, with the myriad details of the world. They live in the "jungle." What fascinates them is the uniqueness of particular entities, the hard and messy "givenness" of things. They don't care so much how things hang together as what they are really like.[1]

The Christian tradition, continues Garrett, is similarly mixed with thinkers extolling the virtues of either the unifying or the diversifying approach to theology. The former prefer theological systems that integrate the various elements of their thought into a consistent whole. Thinkers who favor the diversifying approach, however, cast a suspicious eye toward such projects. Some of them have a nagging sense that such grand systems of thought conceal more than they reveal; others believe that such systems are built on presuppositions about the world that are no longer universally shared in today's highly pluralistic world; and still others simply believe that the Christian faith defies the neat, clean categorization such systems seem to require.

We turn our attention now to the first moment in the portion of the biblical narrative that Christians call the New Testament. We take as our theological guide the thinker who was arguably the most important Roman Catholic theologian of the twentieth century: Karl Rahner. We also have in Rahner an example of a great unifying theological mind at work. While his writings covered an amazingly wide range of topics, he carried on those investigations in light of his unifying vision, a grand scheme in which theological questions could be, according to Rahner, most profitably asked and answered. Central to Rahner's inquiry was to ask about the meaning of Christ for contemporary, twenty-first-century Christians. It will fall to the reader to determine whether Rahner ignored the jungle or blazed a trail straight through it.

Biography of Karl Rahner

At his death in 1984, Rahner left behind a body of work that was both enormous in volume and wide ranging in scope. Stanley J. Grenz and Roger E. Olson report, "By 1984 over 3,500 books and articles had appeared in print under [Rahner's] name. His most important articles were collected and published in a twenty-volume set entitled *Theological Investigations*, which contains over eight thousand pages in the German edition."[2]

Born in 1904 in Freiburg, Germany, Rahner was ordained as a Jesuit priest in 1932. Soon after ordination, he began his doctoral studies, but his dissertation was rejected by his adviser. That work, *Spirit in World*, was eventually published and became one of Rahner's most influential works. Rahner began teaching at Innsbruck in 1936, but soon afterward, he was forced to leave Germany when the Nazis closed the school. During World War II, Rahner taught in Vienna, and he finally returned to Innsbruck in 1948.

In the early 1950s, Rahner's essays began to be collected and published in a series under the title *Theological Investigations*. Although Vatican officials looked with suspicion on some of his early writings, Rahner served as a theological adviser to the bishops at the Second Vatican Council in the 1960s. He also assumed the post of professor at the University of Munich and then at Munster.[3]

Rahner's *Theological Investigations*

Rahner was one of the most influential modern Catholic interpreters of the theology of Thomas Aquinas, a thirteenth-century theologian and philosopher. Thomas Aquinas produced a grand, orderly synthesis of Christian belief known as the *Summa Theologiae,* which served as the primary theological text for generations of Roman Catholic seminarians. The ongoing study of his works and the composition of theological works based on his thought comprise a tradition known as *Thomism.*

In 1879, Pope Leo XIII sparked a resurgence in Thomistic studies when he mandated the inclusion of Thomas Aquinas's philosophy in the curriculum of all Catholic seminaries. As scholars became increasingly acquainted with Thomas's original writings, rather than the works of his interpreters, they discovered a rich, original resource for modern Catholic theology. One group of these twentieth-century neo-Thomists sought to integrate Thomas's theology and the modern philosophy of Immanuel Kant.[4] Rahner was one of the most creative theological minds among these so-called transcendental Thomists, and in his *Theological Investigations,* he responded to the theological questions of his day in the method and language of transcendental Thomism.

We will focus on three of Rahner's essays about the incarnation that appeared in *Theological Investigations.* The incarnation, described in the opening chapter of the Gospel of John, is the event of God literally taking on human flesh in the person of Jesus Christ. The reader may operate with a different understanding of Jesus' identity. In theology, one's understanding of Jesus is called a *christology.* Readers may not share Rahner's particular christology, but they will find his views useful in formulating or identifying their own christologies.

With that goal in mind, we will first examine Rahner's approach to theological questions in general and christological questions in particular. We will then delve into Rahner's three essays, each of which helps contemporary readers ponder the essential theological question, What is the meaning of Christ for twenty-first-century Christians?

The first of the three essays we will examine introduces us to Rahner's *transcendental method*. Regarding this method, Robert Kress informs us that "the term and approach have received a definite character from Kant. His description has become normative: the investigation into the conditions presupposed by or necessary for any knowledge."[5] This seems terribly abstract at first, but it simply means that the theologian needs to engage in an orderly method of investigation.

For example, suppose a valuable work of art is stolen from a prestigious museum. Investigators are called to the scene to determine how such a theft could have occurred. They will determine how the security system was bypassed, who had access to the museum, when the crime took place, and so on.

The religious believer accepts on faith that certain events took place in history—for example, that God took on human flesh. Given that fact, the theologian deduces what conditions were necessary for such an event to take place. This requires formulating assumptions about humans (as receivers of God's revelation), history (as the locus of God's revelation), and christology (as the culmination of God's revelation). Kress believes that "in the long run Rahner's transcendental method is a very elaborate explanation of the old scholastic axiom, 'What is received is received according to the mode of the receiver.'"[6] If Kress is correct, then the investigation of God's revelation and the investigation into the human reception of that revelation are two sides of the same coin.

"On the Theology of the Incarnation"

We are now ready to proceed to Rahner's essay "On the Theology of the Incarnation." Rahner begins, "Let us put the simple question: what do we Christians mean when we profess our faith in the incarnation of the Word of God?"[7] Rahner stresses that his work is not to be seen as a departure from the teachings found in the church councils held in Nicaea in 325, in Ephesus in 431, and in Chalcedon in 451.

Rahner begins, "The Word of God became *man*. What does it mean 'became *man*'?"[8] Using the transcendental method, the inquirer could ask, What conditions exist within human nature that make it possible for God to become one with humanity? Rahner's answer is simple: At a minimum, humans have the capacity to know and love God. Further examination of the human subject, however, will reveal an even greater truth: Humans are mysteries. We defy definitive categorization and resolution. "Man is therefore mystery in his essence, his nature. He is not in himself the infinite fullness of mystery which concerns him, for that fullness is inexhaustible, and the primordial form of all that is mystery to us."[9] Humans are mysteries who yearn to know and love God, who is Absolute Mystery.

Rahner turns to the second phase of his investigation. He writes, "The Word of God has *become* man: this is the assertion which we are trying to understand better. We take the word 'become.' Can God 'become' anything?"[10] Here, Rahner insists that Christian faith requires Christ to be fully human and fully divine, not divine in substance but merely human in appearance. "We must therefore regard as heretical any concept of the incarnation which makes the humanity of Jesus only a disguise used by God to signal his challenging presence."[11]

Combining these two phases of the investigation, we can postulate certain preliminary ideas. First, given the fact of the incarnation, we can assume theologically that human nature has the possibility of being assumed by God. There is an innate capacity to receive God's grace. As J. A. Di Noia states, "The message of revelation—the divine self-communication—travels airwaves, so to speak, which are already in place. Revelation does not invade human reality as something utterly alien but as something to which human beings are already in some sense attuned."[12] Second, we can also assume that God's love is the motive for the incarnation, since God would not assume human nature in order to make up some deficiency in God's own nature. As Otto H. Hentz explains,

> To acknowledge the true becoming of God in the human is to confront the mystery of God's creative, self-giving love. Why does God do this, why does God become human? By choice, by will—that is, out of love. The only necessity for God to become in and through an other is the necessity of utterly gratuitous love. The apparently strange idea of God's becoming is really the idea of God's self-giving love.[13]

Third, the unity of two natures in one person suggests that a deeper unity exists between what at first may appear to be conflicting forces. For example, Rahner situates the incarnation in the dynamic interplay between human receptivity and divine activity. Consequently, obedience to God and human fulfillment are united. Rahner writes, "The incarnation of God is therefore the unique, supreme, case of the total actualization of human reality, which consists of the fact that man is in so far as he gives up himself." Similarly, in Christ, divine and human natures are not pitted in battle. Karen Kilby notes,

> Christ can be seen, on Rahner's account, as the radicalization, the supreme case, of what is true of us all. If

to be oriented towards God is what makes us human, then the one who is so oriented towards God that he is utterly given over to God, and taken over by God, is actually the one who is at the same time the most fully human. So the divinity of Christ can be conceived not as the contradiction of Christ's humanity, but as its ultimate fulfillment.[14]

In "On the Theology of the Incarnation," Rahner employs the transcendental method to argue for a fundamental compatibility among anthropology (a view of the human person), theology (view of God), and christology (view of Christ). We turn now to Rahner's attempt to locate the incarnation in the larger scope of human history.

"Christology within an Evolutionary View of the World"

Rahner's starting point in his essay "Christology within an Evolutionary View of the World" is not the mysterious subjective world of the individual but rather the external world studied by biologist and physicists. Rahner's essay can be divided into four parts: an exposition of his working assumptions, observations on the course of natural history, a christology within an evolutionary worldview, and a conclusion.

Rahner identifies five working assumptions. First, the material and the spiritual both originate from God. Second, matter and spirit are not to be seen as diametrically opposed entities but as mutually related elements. The third assumption follows from the first two. Rather than consider matter as opposed to the spirit or as something from which Christians should seek escape, Christians should consider matter as enabling humans to come to a reliable knowledge about the world and even some limited knowledge about God. Fourth, the interplay between matter and spirit is not static; it has a history. Rahner labels this process "active self-transcendence." Furthermore, "this notion of self-transcendence includes also transcendence into what is substantially new, i.e. the leap to a higher *nature*."[15] This belief is expressed in the principle that "the higher order always embraces the lower."[16] Each stage of development requires the earlier stages yet moves beyond them. Fifth, the Christian sees the course of that development in history as interplay between God's offer of grace and the free human response to that offer.

Rahner next offers a theological assessment of the course of natural history, in which "the cosmos gradually becomes conscious of itself."[17] Natural history, on a theological reading, is the history of God's self-communication. This self-communication takes place not apart from the material but in and through the material and decisively in the incarnation.

These preliminary observations converge in Rahner's discussion of the incarnation in the third part of his essay. Rahner offers the following conclusion:

God's communication of himself does not suddenly become uncosmic—directed merely to an isolated, separate subjectivity—but is given to the human race and is historical. This event of self-communication must therefore be thought of as an event which takes place historically in a specifically spatio-temporal manner and which turns to everyone and calls upon their freedom. In other words, this self-communication must have a permanent beginning and must find in this a permanent guarantee of its reality so that it can rightly demand a free decision for the acceptance of this divine self-communication.[18]

Rahner continues, "We give the title Saviour simply to that historical person who, coming in space and time, signifies the beginning of God's absolute communication for all men as something happening irrevocably and which shows this to be happening." Geffrey B. Kelly offers the following summary:

Much of Rahner's mode of doing theology is, therefore, grounded in his conviction that all the dynamics of human life exist in unity within the cosmos and that individual history takes place in the history of Christ and in that of humanity as a whole. For him, the final result of the evolutionary, historical process is still a person's life in God—the very God with whom the people can enjoy a unique relationship in the mystery of God's oneness with them.[19]

In the incarnation, we have the culmination of all that has gone before and the anticipation of all that will be. Modern evolutionary thought, in other words, not only does not exclude the incarnation but in fact provides support for this essential doctrine of Christian faith.

Rahner next argues for the compatibility of his own position with the traditional affirmations of faith. He first turns his attention to the doctrine of the *hypostatic union*. Robert A. Krieg defines this concept as "the uniting of the divine nature and the human nature of Jesus Christ in one person, or *hypostasis* (Gk.). This notion is meant to illumine the mystery of Christ's personal unity, while at the same time safeguarding the Church's insight regarding the mystery of Jesus Christ's two natures, his full divinity and full humanity."[20] In terms of the preservation of Christ's full humanity, Rahner writes,

Seen in this light, it now becomes possible to understand what is really meant by the doctrine of the Hypostatic Union and of the Incarnation of the divine Logos and how, following quite naturally from what has been said, it fits into an evolutionist view of the world. In the first place, the Saviour is himself a historical moment in God's saving action exercised on the world. He is a moment of the history of God's communication of himself to the world—in the sense that he is a part of this history of the cosmos itself. He must not be merely God acting on the world but must be a part of the cosmos itself in its very climax.[21]

In terms of the preservation of Christ's divinity, Rahner insists, "Hence, if the reality in which God's absolute self-communication is pledged and accepted for the whole of humanity and thus becomes 'present' for us (i.e., Christ's reality) is to be really the final and unsurpassable divine self-communication, then it must be said that it is not only posited by God but is God himself."[22] In short, Rahner sees his position in complete continuity with the traditional affirmation that Christ was one person with two natures: one fully human and the other fully divine.[23]

In the final section of his essay, Rahner weighs in on the ancient theological question of whether there would have been an incarnation if there were no sin in the world. Rahner begins, "It should be stated, first of all, that there is quite a long established school of thought among Catholic theologians (usually called the 'Scotist school') which has always stressed that the first and most basic motive for the Incarnation was not the blotting-out of sin but that the Incarnation was already the goal of the divine freedom even apart from any divine fore-knowledge of freely incurred guilt."[24] This debate will most likely strike the modern reader as an example of arcane theologizing, but Rahner believes that seeing the incarnation as a gift of divine self-communication, rather than a remedy for human sinfulness, opens for us a vision of human history as imbued with the presence of God. In other words, incarnation is the *decisive* but necessarily the *exclusive* expression of God's constant concern for the salvation of every human being. A second consequence is that life in this world takes on immense religious significance. "Because man cannot effect his salvation apart from his worldly task but only through it, the latter attains its highest dignity, honour, danger-point and ultimate significance by this very fact."[25]

The reader may wonder, Where is the Jesus who overturned the money changer's tables? Where is the Jesus who suffered anguish in the garden of Gethsemane? In other words, if we change the starting point and begin not with the dogmatic statements of the church (that Jesus is one person with two natures) but with the stories of Jesus found in the gospels, do we arrive at the same conclusion about him?

"The Two Basic Types of Christology"

In his essay "The Two Basic Types of Christology," Rahner distinguishes between a "saving history" type of christology and a metaphysical type of christology.[26] In the former type, Rahner writes, "The eye of the believer in his experience of saving history alights first on the man Jesus of Nazareth, and on him in his fully human reality."[27] The starting point, in other words, is Christ's humanity. The latter, metaphysical type is a descending christology. The starting point here is Christ's divinity. Christ is God in the flesh.

Do these two approaches conflict or produce radically different portraits of Jesus? Not necessarily, argues Rahner. There is a middle ground between the two types, in which a number of christological positions may prove acceptable to the Christian community.

These two types and their mutual interrelationship surely enable us to understand that in present-day Christian theology too there is room for a pluralism of christologies. If these christologies respect the Church's credal formulae concerning Christ where these are definitive, and constantly submit afresh to critical reappraisal by standards outside themselves, and provided that at the same time they include, and accord all due respect to, essential reference to Jesus as the bringer of eschatological salvation, the different christologies can continue to be different, and still be orthodox.[28]

Tyron Inbody regards this attempt to unite these two approaches in christology as one of the most important appealing features of Rahner's theology. He writes, "[Rahner's] effort at unifying this double strand of the christological tradition must stand as one of the high-water marks of his theology."[29]

Rahner's Spiritual Vision

What are some of the essential features of the worldview Rahner develops in the course of his christological investigations? Three of the most important features are the universality of grace, the centrality of Christ, and the sacramentality of the created order.

First, God's grace is universally present. It is present at every turn. The material and spiritual world are created out of the effusive love of God. The incarnation reveals God's intimate, ongoing relationship with the world and stands as God's pledge to that world that its final consummation rests with God. God's grace overflows every boundary we humans erect (even the limits of the Christian religion). Rahner once summarized his view in the following straightforward manner: "I really only want to tell the reader something very simple. Human persons in every age, always and everywhere, whether they realize it and reflect upon it or not, are in relationship with the unutterable mystery of human life that we call God."[30]

The second feature is the centrality of Christ. Rahner's transcendental method does not begin with features about the world and then move into how Christ fits into those features. Instead, the process begins with the incarnation and then hypothesizes about the conditions that must have been present for that event to have occurred. Christ is the starting point. Christ is the definitive expression of God's continuous love for the world (John 3:16). Christ is the irrevocable pledge for the future.

Third, Rahner rejects any understanding of the world that too radically separates matter and spirit or nature and grace. Just as in the hypostatic union, there is a distinction but not a separation between Jesus' humanity and divinity, there is a union of the natural history of the human race and the history of salvation. Richard McBrien argues that "no theological principle or focus is more characteristic of Catholicism or more central to its identity than the principle of *sacramentality*. The Catholic vision sees God in and through all things: other people, communities, movements, events, places, objects, the world at large, the whole cosmos. The visible, the tangible, the finite, the historical—all these are actual or potential carriers of the divine presence."[31] Here, Rahner maintains the tradition of Ignatius of Loyola, the founder of the Jesuits, who encouraged Christians to "find God in all things."

Assessments of Rahner's *Theological Investigations*

We will focus on the three criticisms that Rahner's supporters seem most eager to refute. The first centers on the issue of the uniqueness of Jesus; the second questions whether Rahner has given sufficient attention to the cross; and the third charges that Rahner's presuppositions are outdated.

John McDermott raises the first objection clearly and forcefully in his review of Rahner's claim for the compatibility between human freedom and the omnipotence of God. McDermott writes,

> Just as subject and predicate are unified in a sentence without surrendering their diversity, so divine omnipotence and human freedom are joined while retaining their difference. Indeed, the greater the unity, for Rahner, the

clearer is the difference. Thus he saw in the full, greatest possible actuation of Jesus' freedom the greatest possible union with God, indeed, what the word "Incarnation" intends. But does this universal principle regarding God and man mark the uniqueness of Jesus? Why is it not possible for another human being to accomplish the total surrender to God ascribed to Jesus?[32]

McDermott asks, Why is it not possible for another human being to accomplish the total surrender to God ascribed to Jesus? Denise Carmody and John Carmody, in a very favorable review of Rahner's christology, seem to inadvertently raise the same question:

> To be sure there is a uniqueness in the quality and intensity of the union that Jesus has with God his Father, and "hypostatic union" retains a worth by signaling this uniqueness, this soleness in Jesus' divinization. But what happens in the Incarnation happens, to a considerable degree, whenever any human being accepts God's love, for the dynamics of that love are such, in its incorporation of human beings into the "Body of Christ" and its bestowal of the Spirit, that it works an "assumption" of our human natures into the divine life that is at least analogous to the Logos' assumption of a human nature born of Mary.[33]

This seems to undercut the foundational claim that Christ is the Absolute Savior that Rahner contends he is upholding.

The second criticism concerns Rahner's treatment of the cross in his christology. Rahner insists that the incarnation is not to be regarded as a remedy to human sinfulness but as the highest expression of God's self-communication to the world. McDermott comments, "In such a panhistoric view one might well ask how Jesus' death actually accomplished anything new for man in history; for everything had been determined before creation by the immutable God."[34] Harvey D. Egan writes, "God is unchanging love. God loves even sinful humanity and offers himself even prior to Jesus' actual sacrifice on the cross but in view of it because creation is Christocentric from the very beginning. Because God loves the sinner and wishes to reconcile us to him (not vice versa), the cross, in Rahner's view, is the symbol of God's irrevocable will to communicate himself to us as unconditional love."[35] Critics charge that this simply does not agree with the scriptural claims that we are saved by Christ's death, or, put more formally, critics believe that the cross must always be seen as the cause, not the effect, of our salvation.

The third and final criticism is that Rahner's operating assumptions are no longer widely shared by thinkers in the Western world. J. A. Di Noia offers a balanced summary of this objection:

But Rahner's enthusiastic, if critical, embrace of modernity entwines the fortunes of his theological program with those of specific modern conceptualities which are themselves under attack. It was Rahner's contention that Catholic theology must appropriate the transcendental, anthropological and subjective turns characteristic of modern thought. Thus, in an intellectual climate in which philosophers and theologians are increasingly critical of precisely these elements of modern thought, Rahner's theological program will seem wedded to outmoded interests and conceptions.[36]

This criticism brings us full circle. In the opening paragraph of this chapter, we contrasted theologians who see mountains with those who see jungles. The former, like Rahner, prefer grand systems of thought that integrate and relate the various elements of Christian belief. The latter praise diversity and proceed in a more ad hoc manner. The great revelatory moments for the unifiers are creation and the incarnation. The decisive moment for the iconoclastic diversifiers is the crucifixion.

The Future of Neo-Thomism

At the core of Thomistic theology is the issue of God's grace, which Rahner defines as God's self-communication to humanity. In other words, how is God present to human beings and in what ways does God's activity transform the human person?

For Christians, this is a critically important theological question that concerns the very nature of God, but it is also a spiritually vital question worth pondering. Our conception of grace has implications for how we relate faith and reason, psychology and theology, and matter and spirit. The future viability of neo-Thomism may rest with its ability to demonstrate that these realms are not as separate and distinct as we may believe.

Conclusion

Rahner's essays in *Theological Investigations* view Christian thought and practice through the lens of the incarnation. The theologian we will discuss in the next chapter, Jürgen Moltmann, approaches Christian thought and practice through the lens of the crucifixion. These contrasting starting points generate different engagements with the issues confronting contemporary theologians and as such provide us with an illustration of the richness and diversity of contemporary Christian theology.

Discussion Questions

1. Is it possible to organize all Christian beliefs into a grand system in which the various beliefs relate to each other in an orderly fashion?

2. Do you believe that Christ was one person with two natures: one fully human and the other fully divine?

Is this the standard by which all christologies should be measured?

3. Does the modern evolutionary worldview support or undermine traditional affirmations about Christ?

4. Would the incarnation have taken place if sin never entered the world?

5. Do non-Christians know as much about God's grace as Christians?

6. In theory, could another human be equal to Christ in terms of openness to doing God's will?

7. What is more important to Christian faith: the incarnation or the crucifixion? Why?

⊚ Notes

1. Graeme Garrett, *God Matters: Conversations in Theology* (Collegeville, Minn.: Liturgical Press, 1999), pp. 3–4.

2. Stanley J. Grenz and Roger E. Olson, *Twentieth-Century Theology* (Downers Grove, Ill.: InterVarsity Press, 1992), p. 240.

3. See Thomas O'Meara, "Rahner, Karl," in Richard P. McBrien, ed., *The HarperCollins Encyclopedia of Catholicism* (San Francisco: HarperCollins, 1995).

4. See Gerald A. McCool, *The Neo-Thomists* (Milwaukee: Marquette University Press, 1994), pp. 119–124, where he discusses the approach of Rahner's teacher, Joseph Marechal.

5. Robert Kress, *A Rahner Handbook* (Atlanta: John Knox Press, 1982), p. 27.

6. Kress, *Rahner Handbook*, p. 78.

7. Karl Rahner, "On the Theology of the Incarnation," in *Theological Investigations*, vol. 4 (Baltimore: Helicon Press, 1966), p. 105.

8. Rahner, "On the Theology," p. 107.

9. Ibid., p. 108.

10. Ibid., p. 112.

11. Ibid., pp. 117–118.

12. J. A. Di Noia, "Karl Rahner," in David F. Ford, ed., *The Modern Theologians*, 2nd ed. (Oxford: Blackwell, 1997), p. 124.

13. Otto H. Hentz, "Anticipating Jesus Christ: An Account of Our Hope," in Leo J. O'Donovan, ed., *A World of Grace* (New York: Seabury Press, 1980), p. 117.

14. Karen Kilby, *Karl Rahner* (London: Fount Paperbacks, 1997), p. 19.

15. Karl Rahner, "Christology within an Evolutionary View of the World," in *Theological Investigations*, vol. 5, trans. Karl-H. Kruger (Baltimore: Helicon Press, 1966), p. 165.

16. Rahner, "Christology within an Evolutionary View," p. 167.

17. Ibid., p. 171.

18. Ibid., p. 174.

19. Geffrey B. Kelly, "Introduction," in *Karl Rahner: Theologian of the Graced Search for Meaning* (Minneapolis: Fortress Press, 1992), p. 55.

20. Robert A. Krieg, "Hypostatic Union," in *HarperCollins Encyclopedia of Catholicism*, ed. Richard P. McBrien (San Francisco: HarperCollins, 1995), p. 647.

21. Rahner, "Christology within an Evolutionary View," p. 176.

22. Ibid., p. 183.

23. For a helpful discussion of this particular feature of Rahner's theology, see James J. Buckley, "Karl Rahner as a Dogmatic Theologian," *Thomist* 47 (1983): 364–394.

24. Rahner, "Christology within an Evolutionary View," p. 184.

25. Ibid., p. 191.

26. Karl Rahner, "The Two Basic Types of Christology," in *Theological Investigations*, vol. 13 (New York: Crossroad, 1983), pp. 213–223.

27. Rahner, "Two Basic Types," p. 215.

28. Ibid., p. 222.

29. Tyron Inbody, "Rahner's Christology: A Critical Assessment," *St. Luke's Journal of Theology* 25, no. 4 (1982): 306.

30. Karl Rahner, in Paul Imhof and Hubert Biallowons, eds., *Dialogue: Conversations and Interviews, 1965–1982* (New York: Crossroad, 1986), p. 147. I discovered this quote in Grenz and Olson, *Twentieth-Century Theology*, p. 240.

31. Richard P. McBrien, *Catholicism*, rev. ed. (San Francisco: HarperCollins, 1994), p. 1196.

32. John M. McDermott, "The Christologies of Karl Rahner," *Gregorianum* 67 (1986): 122. For a fascinating book-length survey

of the question of Jesus' uniqueness, see Scott Cowdell, *Is Jesus Unique?* (Mahwah, N.J.: Paulist Press, 1996).

33. Denise Carmody and John Carmody, "Christology in Karl Rahner's Evolutionary World View," *Religion in Life* 49, no. 2 (1980): 209.

34. McDermott, "The Christologies of Karl Rahner," p. 323.

35. Harvey D. Egan, *Karl Rahner: The Mystic of Everyday Life* (New York: Crossroad, 1998), p. 135.

36. Di Noia, "Karl Rahner," p. 131.

◉ Suggested Readings

For a detailed introduction to the scriptural material on the incarnation, see James D. G. Dunn, *Christology in the Making* (Philadelphia: Westminster, 1980).

For background on Thomism, see Rik Van Nieuwenhove and Joseph Wawrykow, eds., *The Theology of Thomas Aquinas* (Notre Dame, Ind.: University of Notre Dame Press, 2005).

For a shorter yet helpful introduction to Rahner's theology, see any of the following: Anne Carr, "Karl Rahner," in Dean G. Peerman and Martin E. Marty, eds., *A Handbook of Christian Theologians*, enlarged ed. (Nashville, Tenn.: Abingdon Press, 1984); chapter 8 of Stanley J. Grenz and Roger E. Olson, *Twentieth-Century Theology* (Downers Grove, Ill.: InterVarsity Press, 1992); J. A. Di Noia, "Karl Rahner," in David F. Ford, ed., *The Modern Theologians*, 2nd ed. (Oxford: Blackwell, 1997); Geffrey B. Kelly, "Introduction," in *Karl Rahner: Theologian of the Graced Search for Meaning* (Minneapolis: Fortress Press, 1992); Karl Lehmann, "Introduction," in *The Content of Faith* (New York: Crossroad, 1992); and chapter 2 of Robert Kress, *A Rahner Handbook* (Atlanta: John Knox Press, 1982).

For a shorter yet helpful introduction to Rahner's christology, see any of the following: chapter 5 of William V. Dych, *Karl Rahner* (Collegeville, Minn.: Liturgical Press, 1992); chapter 2 of Karen Kilby, *Karl Rahner* (London: Fount Paperbacks, 1997); chapter 6 of Harvey D. Egan, *Karl Rahner: Mystic of Everyday Life* (New York: Crossroad, 1998); chapter 5 of Michael Skelley, *The Liturgy of the World: Karl Rahner's Theology of Worship* (Collegeville, Minn.: Liturgical Press, 1991). See also Rahner's "I Believe in Jesus Christ: Interpreting an Article of Faith" (*Theo. Investigations*, vol. 9).

Chapter 7

Crucifixion: Jürgen Moltmann and Political Theology

What is the meaning of Christ's death?

✎*Looking Ahead:*

Jürgen Moltmann (1926–) fought for Germany in World War II and was imprisoned for many years after the war ended. Though he did not have a religious upbringing, his experiences during the war and his encounters with others introduced him to Christianity through the Bible with remarkable force. His questions in theological study, which situate him in the field of political theology, compel new ways of thinking about the core reality of Christianity: the crucified God and the hope of the Resurrection. His theology understands that God is in the world and is affected by the world, which raises questions about theology in a political world. Note that he considers his theology one of exploration, and see in your reading how he encourages personal reflection and inspiration.

At the beginning of the previous chapter, we included Karl Rahner in a group of thinkers labeled "unifiers" who looked for the grand overarching structure into which the various theological beliefs could be placed, related, and ultimately joined. The contrasting approach was labeled "diversifying." Graeme Garrett writes,

Diversifiers are also suspicious of too much consistency. Since when were things humans, especially things religious, consistent? Paul's writing is full of inconsistency. "I do not understand my own actions. For I do not do what I want, I do the very thing I hate" (Rom 7:15). "My strength is made perfect in weakness" (2 Cor 12:9). It is hard to avoid this kind of oxymoron if you take seriously a theo-logy of the cross, that is, the essence of God revealed in the death of a criminal.[1]

We turn now to that death and its theological significance. In this moment of the biblical narrative, it seems that the diversifying approach seems the most appropriate, for at the cross, we see not rationality and order but cruelty and horror. What, then, is the meaning of Christ's death? Our investigation begins with the scriptural claims about the significance of Christ's death and then moves into a discussion of Jürgen Moltmann's *The Crucified God*.

Biblical Background

Jesus of Nazareth was crucified at Golgotha (Calvary, in Latin) by Roman authorities on the charge that he claimed to be "the King of the Jews." While this teaching about the event is an essential part of early Christian preaching, the questions it raises have occupied Christian thinkers for two millennia. For example, Paul writes in his letter to the Romans:

> For while we were still weak, at the right time Christ died for the ungodly. Indeed, rarely will anyone die for a righteous person—though perhaps for a good person someone might actually dare to die. But God proves his love for us in that while we still were sinners Christ died for us. Much more surely then, now that we have been justified by his blood, will we be saved through him from the wrath of God. For if while we were enemies,

we were reconciled to God through the death of his Son, much more surely, having been reconciled, will we be saved by his life. (Romans 5:6-10)

The interpreter could pursue any number of possible lines of inquiry. One could ask about Paul's understanding of the human situation prior to Christ's death. What was Paul's understanding of human sinfulness? How able are we to save ourselves from that sinfulness? A second set of questions could center around Paul's understanding of Christ's death. Did Christ have to be crucified? What does it mean to say Christ died "at the right time"? A third set of questions could focus on the effect of Christ's death. What does it mean to say that "we have been justified by his blood"? How does Christ's death affect us now, centuries later?

The first set of questions deals with human sinfulness. Christ's death is a remedy to a problem. The most common biblical designation for that problem is sin. Sin functions as an umbrella concept, under which other problems may be discussed, including death (1 Corinthians 15:26), the fear of death (Hebrews 2:15), Satan (2 Corinthians 11), principalities and powers (Colossians 2:14), and darkness (1 John 1:7). All these are conditions of the fallen, sinful world. Christ is the solution to the problem of sin. As Paul writes in 2 Corinthians, "For our sake he made him to be sin who knew no sin, so that in him we might become the righteousness of God" (5:21).

The second set of questions deals with the role of the cross. John P. Galvin speaks of three major early Christian assessments of Jesus' death: the death of a prophet-martyr, the death of a righteous sufferer, and the death of an atoning redeemer.[2] In the first instance, Christ stands in a long line of prophets who were persecuted and/or executed for their bold proclamations. In the second portrait, the righteous one suffers persecution for the sake of the unrighteous. It is the third portrait that has occupied much of Christian theology over the last two thousand years. In it, the right-eous one suffered for us and, in doing so, won a victory f or us.

The third set of questions asks specifically about the effect of Christ's death. In the passage from Romans, Paul speaks of our justification, reconciliation, and salvation. This change in ourselves was brought about by Christ's death ("by his blood"). The same teaching is found else-where in the New Testament (1 John 2:2, 1 Peter 3:18, and Hebrews 9:11-28). Paul locates this atonement in the context of God's love. Again, this prompts a series of questions: In what sense is the crucifixion a display of God's love? Is God wrathful? Could Christ have saved us without dying on the cross?

Interpreting other biblical passages dealing with Christ's death involves, in some way, these three sets of questions. For example, in Mark's gospel, Jesus announces that "the Son of Man came not to be served but to serve, and to give his life [as] a ransom for many" (10:45). The metaphor of a ransom is a provocative one; it suggests that Christ paid the price for our release from sin. While this is good news, indeed, it also raises a host of questions: To whom was the ransom paid? If it was paid to the Father, did the Father sac-rifice the Son? If it was paid to Satan, does this represent a victory for the Devil? How did that act of ransoming effect salvation for those born centuries later?

It seems, therefore, that at least three elements must be included in any complete biblical understanding of the death of Christ. First, it was an event that involved pro-found, genuine human suffering. The church has wisely resisted any effort to say that Jesus only appeared to be human and consequently only seemed to suffer. Second, Christ's suffering and death on the cross was not without benefit. It brought about salvation for others, a decisive victory over Satan, and a reconciliation. Paul insists that "Christ died for our sins" (1 Corinthians 15:3). Third, it was part of God's plan for the world. Again, Paul insists that Christ died for us "in accordance with the scriptures" (1 Corinthians 15:3). In both Luke and Acts of the Apostles, where we find no developed theology of the cross, there is nonetheless the sense of the necessity of Christ's death (see Luke 17:25; 24:26). In Acts, Peter announces, "This man, handed over to you according to the definite plan and foreknowledge of God, you crucified and killed by the hands of those outside the law" (2:23).

Theologians have struggled mightily to devise theories that do justice to all three aspects of the biblical proclamation. Anselm of Canterbury, an eleventh-century Christian philosopher, constructed the argument that has probably generated the most attention. Most commentators see Anselm's argument as reflective of the feudal times in which he lived, with its hierarchical understanding of social orders and their respective duties and obligations. Anselm understood human sin to be a dishonor against God. Since humans were the offending party, justice required that humans make the proper satisfaction to God. However, since humans already owed everything to God, they were incapable of offering the proper satisfaction. Humans *needed* to offer the satisfaction, but only God *was able* to offer the satisfaction. Therefore, a God-man was needed to offer the perfect satisfaction for human sinfulness to God.

Trevor Hart makes the following observation at the close of his discussion of Anselm's theory: "If there is a striking omission in Anselm's account of the cross, it is his failure to press beyond the categories of Creator and creature, and to read it as an event in a relationship between a Father and a Son, a dimension which would have provided his basic understanding with an even keener edge, and perhaps set it safely beyond the bounds of misconstrual in terms of a penal exaction model."[3]

We turn now to a theologian who has attempted to do just that: see Christ's death on the cross not as an exchange required by justice but as an event between the Father and the Son.

Biography of Jürgen Moltmann

As was true with the biography of Dietrich Bonhoeffer, that of Jürgen Moltmann sheds light on his theology. He was born in Hamburg, Germany, in 1926. As a young man fighting in the German army during World War II, he was captured and held as a prisoner of war in camps in Belgium and Scotland.[4] In a piece written more than fifty years after his capture, Moltmann compared his own time in the camps to Jacob's struggle with the angel (Genesis 32). Moltmann recounts,

> In the years I spent as a prisoner of war, 1945–1948, the biblical story about Jacob's struggle with the angel of the Lord at the Jabbok was for me always the story about God in which I found again my own little human story. . . .
> We were caught up in the terrors of the end of the war, and in the hopeless misery of a prisoner of war's existence. We wrestled with God in order to survive in the abysses of senselessness and guilt and we emerged from those years "limping" indeed, but blessed. The end of the war, when it at last came, found us with deeply wounded souls; but after the years in the Norton prisoner-of-war camp in Scotland many of us said: "My soul has been healed, for I have seen God."[5]

Moltmann describes the low point of imprisonment:

And then came what was the worst of all. In September 1945, in Camp 22 in Scotland, we were confronted with pictures of Belsen and Auschwitz. They were pinned up in one of the huts, without comment. Some people thought it was propaganda. Others set the piles of bodies which they saw over against Dresden. But slowly and inexorably the truth filtered into our awareness, and we saw ourselves mirrored in the eyes of the Nazi victims. Was this what we had fought for? Had my generation, at the last, been driven to our deaths so that the concentration camp murderers could go on killing, and Hitler could live a few months longer?[6]

Moltmann's spiritual rejuvenation came from two sources: the kindness of other people, including the local Scots and English who extended hospitality to the prisoners of war, and the Bible. Moltmann's upbringing was not especially religious, but when he began to read the psalms of lament (especially Psalm 39), he was struck to the core. More importantly for this present investigation, the passion of Christ proved particularly illuminating.

Then I came to the story of the passion, and when I read Jesus' death cry, "My God, why have you forsaken me?" I knew with certainty: this is someone who understands you. I began to understand the assailed Christ because I felt that he understood me: this was the divine brother in distress, who takes the prisoners with him on his way to the resurrection. I began to summon up the courage to live again, seized by a great hope. I was even calm when other men were "repatriated" and I was not. This early fellowship, the brother in suffering and the redeemer from guilt, has never left me since. I never "decided for Christ" as is often demanded of us, but I am sure that then and there, in the dark pit of my soul, he found me. Christ's godforsakenness showed me where God is, where he had been with me in my life, and where he would be in the future.[7]

With this background, we can now turn our attention to Moltmann's theology of the cross. It is a theology about grief and forsakenness but ultimately liberation.

Moltmann's *The Crucified God*

Our investigation of *The Crucified God* will focus on three areas: the foundational claims asserted by Moltmann, Moltmann's theology of the cross, and the interpersonal and social implications of the cross.

Foundational Claims

Three of Moltmann's foundational claims are of particular importance to us in this present investigation. The first is methodological, the second philosophical, and the third christological.

First, Moltmann believes the task confronting contemporary theologians is to construct a Christian theology that is both relevant to the lives of people yet preserves their identity as Christians. Moltmann suggests that too often, theologians choose one to the exclusion of the other. He asserts, however, that a theology of the cross captures both aspects. By keeping the crucified Christ as the "inner criterion of theology" and a theology of the cross as "the key signature for all Christian theology," Christian theologians will preserve their identity as Christians while speaking meaningfully to the "despised, abandoned, and oppressed" of the world.[8]

The second foundational claim deals with epistemology—the study of knowledge. The ancient principle of "Like is known only by like" explains how humans come to the knowledge of truth. For Plato, the immortal soul recognizes the truth that it knew before it was joined with a human body. In that way, knowledge is actually recollection. If like is known by like, continues this line of reasoning, an analogy discloses truth by enabling us to see the similarities between the two objects in the comparison. It is what helps Christians understand the meaning of the psalmist's poetic assertion that "the Lord is my shepherd" (Psalm 23). Moltmann, however, argues that truth can also be discovered in dissimilarity.

This analogical principle of knowledge is one-sided if it is not supplemented by the dialectic principle of knowledge. This principle derives from medicine, going back to Hippocrates, and states that *contraria contrariis curantur*, or, in Schelling's words: "Every being can be revealed only in its opposite. Love only in hatred, unity only in conflict." Applied to Christian theology, this means that God is only revealed as "God" in his opposite: godlessness and abandonment by God.[9]

Despite our best efforts to understand the crucifixion, the cross remains "a stumbling block to Jews and foolishness to Gentiles, but to those who are called, Jews and Greeks, Christ is the power of God and the wisdom of God" (1 Corinthians 1:23-24).

The third foundational claim is christological in nature. Here again, we find a dual focus. Christology must engage in historical investigation to better understand the biblical proclamation about Christ, yet it must speak in a meaningful way to the situation of Christians living in the world today. If attention is focused exclusively on the former goal, then the christology may be faithful to Scripture but ineffective as an agent for social change. If attention is focused exclusively on the latter goal, however, then the scriptural moorings will be torn loose.

Theology of the Cross

In the sixth chapter of *The Crucified God*, Moltmann constructs a theology (an understanding of God) that is remarkably traditional in some aspects and utterly revolutionary in others. It is traditional in the sense that is thoroughly trinitarian. In the modern age, many theologians have minimized the role of the Trinity in their thinking. The great father of Protestant liberalism, Friedrich Schleiermacher, did not address the Trinity until the conclusion in his *magnum opus*,

The Christian Faith. Moltmann, by contrast, sees the Trinity as essential to Christian faith.

Moltmann's first revolutionary perspective is to see the crucifixion as an inner trinitarian event between the Father and the Son. Moltmann states that "what happened on the cross was an event between God and God. It was a deep division in God himself, in so far as God abandoned God and contradicted himself, and at the same time a unity in God, in so far as God was at one with God and corresponded to himself."[10] As Moltmann explains,

> To understand what happened between Jesus and his God and Father on the cross, it is necessary to talk in trinitarian terms. The Son suffers dying, the Father suffers the death of the Son. The grief of the Father here is just as important as the death of the Son. The Fatherlessness of the Son is matched by the Sonlessness of the Father, and if God has constituted himself as the Father of Jesus Christ, then he also suffers the death of his Fatherhood in the death of the Son.[11]

Moltmann charges that by focusing on the cross as an event of salvation for humanity, theologians have overlooked the critical question, "What does the cross of Jesus mean for God himself?"[12] Moltmann concludes, "In the cross, Father and Son are most deeply separated in forsakenness and at the same time are most inwardly one in their surrender. What proceeds from this event between Father and Son is the Spirit which justifies the godless, fills the forsaken with love and even brings the dead alive."[13] In other words, the cross is the supreme manifestation of the "inner-trinitarian tensions and relationships of God."[14] In more provocative terms, "Anyone who really talks of the Trinity talks of the cross of Jesus, and does not speculate in heavenly riddles."[15]

Moltmann's second revolutionary concept is to speak of "the grief of the Father." For Moltmann, the concept of

God's grief captures more faithfully the dynamism of the biblical language about God. Moltmann argues that much of early Christian theology was shaped by the prevailing Greek patterns of thought that regarded suffering or emotion as signs of instability and imperfection. Moltmann believes that "the time has finally come for differentiating the Father of Jesus Christ from the God of the pagans and the philosophers (Pascal) in the interest of Christian faith."[16] The God of Jesus Christ, insists Moltmann, loves, rejoices, and grieves—in short, is a God of pathos, not apathy.

This leads us to the third of Moltmann's revolutionary concepts: the history of God. The history of the world, including its suffering, is "taken up in God." In an earlier discussion of Moltmann's biography, we read about his reaction to the pictures of Belsen and Auschwitz that were posted on the walls of the camp in which he was confined as a prisoner of war. In light of that fact, the following passage is especially significant. He writes, "It must also be said that, like the cross of Christ, even Auschwitz is in God himself. Even Auschwitz is taken up into the grief of the Father, the surrender of the Son and the power of the Spirit. That never means that Auschwitz and other grisly places can be justified, for it is the cross that is the beginning of the trinitarian history of God."[17] Between the present and the future culmination of this trinitarian history of God, there is hope: the virtue that sustains our faith and allows us to love.

The Interpersonal and Social Implications of the Cross

Moltmann concludes *The Crucified God* with a discussion of psychological and social liberation. Christians are called to act in the present in ways that reflect their beliefs about the end of time. Moltmann is quite specific about what he sees as the "vicious circles of death" and what social, economic, and political commitments are needed to break through each of those circles. Moltmann includes in his list of "vicious circles of death" the following: poverty, force, racial and cultural alienation, industrial pollution, senselessness, and godforsakenness. By way of providing a concrete guide for liberation, Moltmann advocates the following commitments that correspond to each of the various woes he has listed: socialism, democracy, cultural emancipation, peace with nature, and a general commitment to human welfare.

Assessments of Moltmann's *The Crucified God*

We will examine two criticisms of Moltmann's theology, as presented in *The Crucified God*. The first criticism focuses on Moltmann's concept of God; the second charges that he operates with a truncated view of revelation.

The first charge that we will explore is that Moltmann makes God in some way dependent on the world for God to be the triune God. Stanley J. Grenz and Roger E. Olson offer the following observation:

> Given Moltmann's adamant insistence that Jesus' cross and resurrection as well as the sending of the Spirit to the church constitute the trinitarian life of God, his "trinitarian history of the cross" naturally raises a crucial question: Would God be trinitarian apart from the events of the world history?
>
> In *The Crucified God* Moltmann seemed to deny any eternal triune life of God already constituted apart from the event of the cross: "Anyone who really talks of the Trinity talks of the cross of Jesus and does not speculate in heavenly riddles." This appears to be a thorough rejection of the traditional [view of God] . . . as existing in triune heavenly perfection from all eternity.[18]

Richard Bauckham puts the matter this way:

> It seems that it would be less accurate to say that Moltmann's God is love than that he becomes love. . . . Moltmann so concentrates on God's involvement with his creation as virtually to make that involvement his whole being. So in the event of the cross in which God's love for the godless is enacted a change in God is revealed. In the process of salvation history God not only reveals himself but actually becomes himself.[19]

This concept of a change in God leads us to Moltmann's contention that God is grieved by the death of Christ. In his treatment of God's grief, Moltmann's uses language that is reminiscent of the ancient belief known as *patripassianism:* "(Lat., 'the suffering of the Father'), the belief that, in Christ's suffering and death, God suffered and died."[20] Moltmann believes he has avoided the charge of patripassianism by distinguishing between the suffering of the Father and the suffering of the Son. However, Carl Braaten criticizes Moltmann on this point:

> Although Moltmann wishes to give real substance to his metaphor of "the crucified God," in the end he draws away from patripassianism. But can Moltmann have it both ways, both that there is any real meaning to his chosen phrase "the crucified God"—which incidentally is an untrinitarian way of speaking—and that his teaching is not patripassianist? . . . In what sense is it or is it not patripassianist when he speaks of the "infinite grief of the Father" in the death of his Son? . . . Why be afraid of patripassianism? Why not meet it head-on if one seriously hopes to challenge the old Greek philosophical concept of God that placed restrictions on the more passionate language of God in the Bible?[21]

John Macquarrie, who believes that *The Crucified God* "would have a good claim to be regarded as possibly the most important theological book to be published in the second half of the twentieth century,"[22] argues that Moltmann is locked in a contradiction. Macquarrie remarks,

> But we may note a problematic area in *The Crucified God*. In spite of the tradition of the divine impassibility, Moltmann thinks of God *in* Christ or *with* Christ, even in the passion. But as a concession to the Reformed theological tradition to which he belongs, Moltmann also wants to speak of Jesus as abandoned by God. Jesus, it would appear from his cry of dereliction, did subjectively *feel* himself abandoned. But Moltmann wants to say he really was abandoned, and this is in plain contradiction to his claim that the Father was suffering in and with Jesus.[23]

While Braaten and Macquarrie argue that Moltmann is trying to hold too many positions simultaneously, others believe he does not hold enough positions. This latter assertion leads us to the next criticism of *The Crucified God*.

The second general criticism leveled against *The Crucified God* concerns Moltmann's almost exclusive focus on the cross as the moment of revelation. Ronald D. Zimany offers the following reminder:

> We don't have to wait until Jesus is on the Cross to find the unexpected. His life is filled with the unexpected, from his insistence on the imminence of God's reign, his eating with publicans and sinners, his fraternization with other "unacceptable" people, his recognition of the "full citizenship" of women, and his teaching of righteousness through grace to his claim of personal authority—as Moltmann himself recognizes.[24]

Zimany's complaint reflects many of the same complaints leveled against Karl Rahner on the incarnation.

If a Christian theologian argues that a single moment in Christ's life is the decisive revelatory moment, does not that diminish (and possibly eliminate) the importance of other moments in Christ's life or the importance of Christ's entire life?

In one of his final comments about *The Crucified God,* Braaten raises a similar concern. He writes, "My most serious difficulty is with its overstatement. It suffers from the occupational hazard of systematic theologians in particular—the tyranny of the single category. We are told by Moltmann that the cross is the criterion of *all* theology. *Only* the cross is the test of everything to be called Christian. The cross is *the* center of *all* Christian theology."[25] In fairness to Moltmann, this criticism loses some of its force when we consider the entire corpus of his work, but as a specific criticism of *The Crucified God,* it seems fair.

The Future of Political Theology

Moltmann's three revolutionary concepts—the inner trinitarian dynamics, the emotion of God, and the taking up of human history in God's history—converge in his understanding of the Christian life. Moltmann ends *The Crucified God* with the following summary: "Brotherhood with Christ means the suffering and active participation in the history of this God. Its criterion is the history of the crucified and risen Christ. Its power is the sighing and liberating spirit of God. Its consummation lies in the kingdom of the triune God which sets all things free and fills them with meaning."[26]

Christian theology, according to Moltmann, needs to be animated by "the sighing and liberating spirit of God." Moltmann calls for an explicit recognition of the political dimension of all theological positions. He contends, "There is a theology which is conscious of its own political function; there is also naive, and as it were, politically unconscious theology. But there is no *a*political theology; neither [on] earth nor in heaven."[27] The common beliefs that "Religion is a private affair" and that "Politics and religion should be kept separate" are themselves political statements, according to Moltmann.[28] Both express a political theory of noninvolvement, but they are no less political than calls for activism.

This *political theology* first took root in Germany in the 1960s, with the political and military tension that existed after the building of the Berlin Wall in 1961. With both the United States and the Soviet Union stockpiling nuclear weapons on each side of the so-called iron curtain, theologians began crafting theologies that spoke to the political realities around them. "The new Political Theology," writes Moltmann, "presupposes the *public* witness of faith and the political discipleship of Christ. It does not desire to politicize the Church, as has been accused. Rather, it desires to 'christianize' the political existence of the churches and of individual Christians according to the standard set for the disciples of Christ in the Sermon on the Mount."[29]

Conclusion

The crucifixion is not, of course, the final word in the Christian message. The resurrection, the cornerstone of the Christian faith, is the pivotal event in the theology of our next theologian, Stanley Hauerwas. Where Moltmann focuses on the political activity of Christians in the world, Hauerwas takes a strikingly different stance toward the world.

◉ Discussion Questions

1. Did Christ have to die on the cross? What did Christ accomplish in doing so? Could Christ have accomplished all that he needed to accomplish and not have been crucified?

2. Did the Father grieve over the death of the Son? Do you find language about God suffering appealing or unappealing?

3. What does Moltmann mean when he says that human history is taken up into God's history?

4. Does the cross define most clearly and concretely the nature of God? If so, what is revealed about God at the cross?

5. Is there a connection between the cross and social issues such as poverty and pollution? If so, what is it?

6. Interpret Jesus' words on the cross: "My God, my God, why have you forsaken me?" (Mark 15:34).

7. What is the significance of the crucifixion for those of us who live two thousand years after it occurred?

◉ Notes

1. Graeme Garrett, *God Matters: Conversations in Theology* (Collegeville, Minn.: Liturgical Press, 1999), p. 7.

2. John P. Galvin, "Jesus Christ," in John P. Galvin and Francis Schüssler Fiorenza, eds., *Systematic Theology* (Minneapolis: Fortress Press, 1991), pp. 295–297.

3. Trevor Hart, "Redemption and Fall," in Colin Gunton, ed., *Cambridge Companion to Christian Doctrine* (Cambridge: Cambridge University Press, 1997), p. 201. Hart's complete chapter provides a helpful introduction to the concept of salvation.

4. See Stanley J. Grenz and Roger E. Olson, *Twentieth-Century Theology* (Downers Grove, Ill.: InterVarsity Press, 1992), p. 173.

5. Jürgen Moltmann, "Wrestling with God: A Personal Meditation," *Christian Century* 114, no. 23 (1997): 726.

6. Moltmann, "Wrestling with God," p. 727.

7. Ibid., p. 727.

8. Jürgen Moltmann, *The Crucified God* (San Francisco: Harper & Row, 1974), pp. 7, 72, 24.

9. Moltmann, *The Crucified God,* p. 27.

10. Ibid., p. 244.

11. Ibid., p. 243.

12. Ibid., p. 201.
13. Ibid., p. 244.
14. Ibid., p. 204.
15. Ibid., p. 207.
16. Ibid., p. 215.
17. Ibid., p. 278.
18. Grenz and Olson, *Twentieth-Century Theology*, p. 182. See also Ed. L. Miller and Stanley J. Grenz, *Fortress Introduction to Contemporary Theologies* (Minneapolis: Fortress Press, 1998), pp. 122–123.
19. Richard Bauckham, "Moltmann's Eschatology of the Cross," *Scottish Journal of Theology* 30 (1977): 310.
20. "Patripassianism," in Richard P. McBrien, ed., *HarperCollins Encyclopedia of Catholicism* (San Francisco: HarperCollins, 1995), p. 966.
21. Carl Braaten, "A Trinitarian Theology of the Cross," *Journal of Religion* 56 (1976): 117–118.
22. John Macquarrie, *Jesus Christ in Modern Thought* (Philadelphia: Trinity Press, 1990), p. 321.
23. Macquarrie, *Jesus Christ in Modern Thought*, p. 323.
24. Roland D. Zimany, "Moltmann's Crucified God," *Dialog* 16 (1977): 52.
25. Braaten, "Trinitarian Theology," p. 120. Italics in original.
26. Moltmann, *The Crucified God*, p. 338.
27. Jürgen Moltmann, *On Human Dignity* (Philadelphia: Fortress Press, 1984), p. 99.
28. Jürgen Moltmann, "Political Theology and Liberation Theology," *Union Seminary Quarterly Review* 45 (1991): 207–208.
29. Moltmann, "Political Theology," p. 208. Italics in original.

Suggested Readings

For an excellent scholarly treatment of the crucifixion, see the two-volume work of Raymond E. Brown, *The Death of the Messiah* (New York: Doubleday, 1994).

For an overview of contemporary thinking about salvation, see Trevor Hart, "Redemption and Fall," in Colin E. Gunton, ed., *The Cambridge Companion to Christian Doctrine* (Cambridge: Cambridge University Press, 1997). See also Denis Edwards, *What*

Are They Saying about Salvation? (Mahwah, N.J.: Paulist Press, 1986), and Brennan Hill, *Jesus the Christ* (Mystic, Conn.: Twenty-Third Publications, 1991), chapter 11.

For overviews of Moltmann's theology, see any of the following: Stanley J. Grenz and Roger E. Olson, *Twentieth-Century Theology* (Downers Grove, Ill.: InterVarsity Press, 1992), chapter 6; Richard Bauckham, "Jürgen Moltmann," in *The Modern Theologians*, 2nd ed., ed. David F. Ford (Oxford: Blackwell, 1997); Richard Bauckham, *The Theology of Jürgen Moltmann* (Edinburgh: T & T Clark, 1995); or Ed. L. Miller and Stanley J. Grenz, *Fortress Introduction to Contemporary Theologies* (Minneapolis: Fortress Press, 1998), chapter 8.

For shorter pieces devoted almost exclusively to *The Crucified God*, see any of these works: Richard Bauckham, *The Theology of Jürgen Moltmann* (Edinburgh: T & T Clark, 1995), chapter 3; Richard Bauckham, "Moltmann's Eschatology of the Cross," *Scottish Journal of Theology* 30 (1977): 301–311; Roland D. Zimany, "Moltmann's Crucified God," *Dialog* 16 (1977): 49–57; Don Schweitzer, "Jürgen Moltmann's Theology as a Theology of the Cross," *Studies in Religion* 24, no. 1 (1995): 95–107; or D. G. Attfield, "Can God Be Crucified? A Discussion of J. Moltmann," *Scottish Journal of Theology* 30 (1977): 47–57.

A more difficult but helpful piece is chapter 4 of A. J. Conyers, *God, Hope, and History* (Macon, Ga.: Mercer University Press, 1988).

Chapter 8

Resurrection: Stanley Hauerwas and Postliberal Theology

What does the resurrection mean for Christian life?

> ✧*Looking Ahead*
>
> Stanley Hauerwas (1940–) is a Protestant theologian whose theology is considered part of the postliberal movement, which began in the 1960s. In contrast with liberal theology, which elevates the authority of the individual person in determining what makes sense theologically, postliberals argue the need to recover an understanding of Scripture as authoritative, but understood critically within an historical context. They do not embrace returning to some kind of preliberal, dogmatic approach to religious meaning, but rather place the story of our lives in the broader context of the Christian narrative. Pay attention in this chapter to the importance Hauerwas places on recovering ideas of virtue and character in working through questions of moral Christian living.

The ignominy of Christ's death was surpassed by the glory of his resurrection. So central, in fact, is the resurrection that Paul insists that if Christ has not been raised from the dead, then Christianity is a fraud (see 1 Corinthians 15:13–19). For Christians, the resurrection not only confirms the truth of Christ's earthly ministry, but it also grounds their hope that the future victory over all that is opposed to God's will has been assured.

Over the course of his career, the Christian ethicist Stanley Hauerwas (1940–) has produced a sizable collection of essays, lectures, sermons, and books devoted to describing in rich detail the life of faithful discipleship for Christians—a people who understand themselves to be living between the life, death, and resurrection of Jesus Christ and the end of time. Hauerwas's most systematic presentation of his theological and ethical vision of the Christian life of nonviolence can be found in his 1983 work *The Peaceable Kingdom*.

Biography of Stanley Hauerwas

Born and raised in Texas, Hauerwas grew up in a pious Methodist family. His father, a bricklayer, would serve as a quiet inspiration for much of Hauerwas's later work on the virtues or skills necessary to cultivate a Christian way of life. After graduating from Southwestern University, Hauerwas pursued his graduate work at Yale, where he was taught by George Lindbeck, Hans Frei, and Paul Holmer—thinkers whose work would later come to represent the Yale School of thought, or *postliberalism*. Hauerwas's dissertation argued for the recovery of the neglected issues of virtue and character as important categories for contemporary Christian ethics.

Hauerwas first taught at Augustana College in Illinois before joining the faculty at the University of Notre Dame. His colleague at Notre Dame was John Howard Yoder, a Mennonite theologian whose account of Christ, the church, and the relationship between the church and the wider society would convince Hauerwas that Christian discipleship necessarily involves a commitment to nonviolence. It was during his time at Notre Dame that Hauerwas published *The Peaceable Kingdom*.

In 1984, Hauerwas moved to Duke University. In 2001, *Time* named him "America's Best Theologian." When informed of this distinction, Hauerwas responded characteristically, "Best is not a theological category! Faithful or unfaithful are the right categories. The last thing in the world I'd want to be is the best."[1]

Through his provocative writings and lectures, Hauerwas has influenced a generation of Christian ethicists, as well as interested Christian readers who ask, What does the resurrection mean for Christian life? How do we live as disciples of the resurrected Christ in a morally fragmented world?

The Peaceable Kingdom

In the opening chapter of *The Peaceable Kingdom*, Hauerwas outlines what he believes is the mistaken view many people have regarding the task of Christian ethics. Because we live today in a world in which people hold a wide range of moral positions and offer a dizzying array of reasons for their positions regarding abortion, divorce, homosexuality, and so on, Christians commonly assume that they need to ground their moral positions in universal principles that any reasonable person would find compelling. In this way, Christians can best support the values and moral positions that will create and maintain a more just society. At the same time, Christians should demonstrate how the principles of the gospel coincide with the insights found in the hearts of all thoughtful, ethically minded human beings. The task of Christian ethics, then, is to demonstrate that Christian moral beliefs are grounded in universal principles.[2]

Hauerwas rejects this understanding of Christian ethics. What many ethicists fear is a liability, Hauerwas embraces as an asset for Christian ethical thought. Whereas some ethicists insist that moral positions that lack universality cannot contribute to public debate, Hauerwas suggests that

Christian morality is grounded in a particular "story"—a story narrated in Scripture and continued over time by the Christian community. The church best serves the world not by supporting its values but by helping "the world understand what it means to be the world."[3] Whereas other ethicists insist that genuine moral choice requires the person making the choice to be free from external influence, Hauerwas emphasizes the need for moral character to be shaped by the life of the church. Whereas many ethicists seek to demonstrate the truth of Christian convictions by showing that they are in accordance with the highest demands of human reason or that they are built on rationally certain foundations, Hauerwas locates the truth in the lives of those who skillfully witness to the gospel in their lives.

In the second chapter of *The Peaceable Kingdom*, Hauerwas advances the claim that "every ethic requires a qualifier."[4] All ethical claims are rooted in traditions that shape how we view the world. As Hauerwas argues later, "There is no point outside our history where we can secure a place to anchor our moral convictions."[5] In Hauerwas's terminology, all ethical claims are "narrative dependent."[6] The discipline of *ethics* does not exist, but the disciplines of *Christian ethics, Buddhist ethics,* and *free-market ethics* do. The qualifier describes more accurately the nature of the moral argument.

Here, Hauerwas stands in opposition to such influential eighteenth-century thinkers as Jeremy Bentham and Immanuel Kant. Although Bentham (one of the originators of utilitarianism) and Kant (who formulated the categorical imperative) differed in the content of their ethical theories, they both assumed that the moral life requires the formulation of rules or principles that all rational persons would accept as true. Hauerwas contends that "the attempt to develop an unqualified ethic, with the attending stress on rules and obligations, has resulted in a failure to stress exactly those virtues we need to live in [a world of moral conflicts]."[7] The specific virtues (qualities, skills, habits) that need to be cultivated are also narrative dependent. To do *Christian* ethics, we need to ask what virtues are required for the development of a sound Christian moral character.

The issue of character, which Hauerwas treats in the third chapter of *The Peaceable Kingdom,* is a persistent theme throughout his writings. Character is a readiness and willingness to respond with the necessary skills to properly perform the task before us. Character develops as the self is formed over time. The formation of good moral character, in turn, requires training in a truthful narrative. Hauerwas writes, "We know who we are only when we can place our selves—locate our stories—within God's story."[8] The themes of virtue, character, and narrative reinforce each other. Virtue shapes character. The development of Christian character requires the frank acknowledgment of our past failings and a commitment to constant conversion toward a specific goal (holiness).

Unlike traditional ethicists, who tie the concepts of virtue and character to some general account of human nature (hence, all humans would seek to cultivate the same virtues), Hauerwas roots virtue in the specific story of the life, death, and resurrection of Jesus Christ. For this reason, "Christian ethics is not first of all an ethics of principles, laws, or values, but an ethic that demands we attend to the life of a particular individual—Jesus of Nazareth."[9]

"Jesus: The Presence of the Peaceable Kingdom"

Chapter 5 in Hauerwas's *The Peaceable Kingdom,* entitled "Jesus: The Presence of the Peaceable Kingdom," describes the specific content of an ethic that bears the qualifier *Christian.* In this chapter, we see the tremendous influence of John Howard Yoder's work on Hauerwas's thought. As

Hauerwas commented after Yoder's death in 1997, "Reading Yoder made me a pacifist. It did so because John taught me that nonviolence was not just another 'moral issue' but constitutes the heart of our worship of a crucified messiah."[10] Jesus, Yoder insisted, was the embodiment of God's kingdom of nonresistant love. Jesus preached about that peaceable kingdom, invited his disciples to join him in that kingdom, and witnessed to that kingdom by his crucifixion. The victory of the resurrection was the assurance by God that this kingdom will prevail over the forces of evil. As Hauerwas wrote in one of his early essays,

> According to Yoder the essence of the incarnation is the nonresistant love that reached its most intense reality on the cross. Christ indeed brought a new life that has immense social implications, but all through his life he refused the political means, i.e., coercive techniques, that were offered to him to accomplish his purposes. This was necessary because the very essence of the incarnation, the meaning of the victory of the resurrection, and the subsequent form of the Christian life is that God deals with evil through self-giving nonresistant love.[11]

Hauerwas echoes Yoder's theology when he writes in *The Peaceable Kingdom*, "Thus to be like Jesus is to join him in the journey through which we are trained to be a people capable of claiming citizenship in God's kingdom of nonviolent love—a love that would overcome the powers of this world, not through coercion and force, but through the power of this one man's death."[12]

The ministry of Jesus, insists Hauerwas, comes into clearest focus when viewed through the lens of the crucifixion. As he argues in *A Community of Character*, "The cross was not something accidental in Jesus' life, but the necessary outcome of his life and his mission. His death is of decisive significance not because it alone wrought salvation for us, but because it was the end and fulfillment of his life. In his death he finished the work that it was his mission to perform."[13]

The cross reveals the precise nature of Jesus' messiahship. The cross is Jesus' willing surrender to both the will of God and the violence that fills the world. As such, the cross is "the summary of his whole life."[14] It is also the life to which Jesus summons his disciples (Mark 8:34). Hauerwas suggests that like Peter, who recoiled at the suggestion that Jesus would suffer and die, Christians too often resort to violence in their efforts to secure justice. As Hauerwas provocatively states elsewhere, "One cannot but feel that those who defend so strongly the use of violence in the service of justice are finally trying to rescue Jesus from the cross."[15] The gospel, however, does not end on Good Friday.

The Centrality of the Resurrection

What is the significance of the resurrection for the Christian life? It is, according to Hauerwas, "the absolute center of history."[16] For Hauerwas, the resurrection is both the confirmation of the truth of what Jesus taught in word and deed during his ministry and the basis for the Christian confidence that a life committed to the nonviolent kingdom of God is a life lived according to the will of God.

On the first of these two points, Hauerwas writes, "The resurrection, therefore, is not an extra-ordinary event added to this man's life, but a confirmation by God that the character of Jesus' life prior to the resurrection is perfectly faithful to his vocation to proclaim and make present God's kingdom. Without the resurrection our concentration on Jesus would be idolatry, but without Jesus' life we would not know what kind of God it is who raised him from the dead."[17] With regard to the second point, Hauerwas states, "Only if our Lord is a risen Lord, therefore, can we have the confidence and the power to be a community of forgiveness. . . . [The] resurrection of Jesus is the ultimate sign that our salvation comes only when we cease trying to interpret Jesus' story in the light of our history, and instead we interpret ourselves in light of his."[18]

In a sermon that Hauerwas delivered one Easter Sunday, he insists that interpreting ourselves in light of the resurrection requires that we see ourselves as a people of forgiveness.

> God raised Jesus on the third day changing forever the way things are. No longer is it necessary to live as if there is no alternative to the powers that feed on our fears, our lusts, our hopelessness. There is an alternative kingdom to that rule of darkness—it is called forgiveness. To be forgiven is not to be told that no matter what we may have done or did not do, it is all right with God. No, to be forgiven is to be made part of a community, a history, that would not, could not exist if Jesus were not God's Christ, raised from the dead. To be forgiven means that we are now, through our baptism, given names, names that make it possible for Jesus to call us to recognition.[19]

As Hauerwas notes in *The Peaceable Kingdom*, "Through this crucified but resurrected savior we see that God offers to all the possibility of living in peace by the power of forgiveness."[20]

The Christian gospel proclaims an *eschatological* truth—that is, a truth that was displayed at the resurrection but that will only be fully realized at the end of history. According to Hauerwas, "To begin to understand Jesus' announcement of the kingdom we must first rid ourselves of the notion that the world we experience will exist indefinitely. We must learn to see the world as Israel had learned to understand it—that is, eschatologically."[21] Forgiveness and nonviolence are not pragmatic strategies based on an anticipated return of greater peace in the world. Rather, they are Christian practices that testify to the truth of the kingdom of God as proclaimed and lived by Jesus—a truth that led Jesus to the cross and a truth that was confirmed by the resurrection.

Hauerwas on the Christian Church

The task of the church is to witness to God's peaceable kingdom that has broken into the world through the life, death, and resurrection of Christ. As Hauerwas states, "The first social ethical task of the church is to be the church—the servant community. Such a claim may well sound self-serving until we remember that what makes the church the church is its faithful manifestation of the peaceable kingdom in the world."[22] This understanding of the church has three immediate consequences in terms of the church's stance toward the world, the church's role in history, and the eschatological nature of Christian prayer and worship.

Hauerwas operates with a clear line of theological demarcation between the church and the world. He repeatedly insists that the church best serves the world by being the church and, in doing so, helps the world understand itself as the world. The church provides a "contrast model" to the life of "the world."[23] As Hauerwas explains in *A Community of Character*, "The world cannot be the church, for the world, while still God's good creation, is a realm that knows not God and is thus characterized by the fears that constantly fuel the fires of violence."[24] By insisting that the church's primary duty is to be the church, Hauerwas wants to overturn the assumption that the Christian church's primary social obligation is to establish a just social order or to inject religious values into debates of public policy. These tasks are not necessarily excluded from the responsibilities of the church, but they are not believed to be its primary mission.

Hauerwas's understanding of the church's role in the world strikes some of his critics as an abdication of its responsibility to contribute to the spiritual and moral well-being of the world. Christians should "seek not so much to be effective as to be faithful" to God, Hauerwas insists.[25] He further stresses that "we do not assume that our task as Christians is to make history come out right."[26] Christian history is filled with attempts to reconcile human free will with God's knowledge and power. Some theories present God and humanity as involved in a cooperative effort to build a better world; others emphasize the sovereignty of God and the need for human obedience to God's will. Hauerwas's approach falls into the latter group.[27] Christians are called to faithfulness and "must assume God will use our faithfulness to make his kingdom a reality in the world."[28]

The church, then, stands as a witness in the world to the action of God. The church lives between the resurrection and the end of time. The church cultivates patience and hope, because it knows that God's victory over evil has been secured by the death and resurrection of Christ. The church is called to be "a foretaste of the peaceable kingdom" and celebrates that reality in the eucharist.[29] The eucharist expresses the unity of the church as the Body of Christ, celebrates the presence of Christ in the world, and anticipates the full realization of God's peaceable kingdom, when former enemies will be reconciled.

Assessments of Hauerwas's The Peaceable Kingdom

One of Hauerwas's most prominent critics, the ethicist James Gustafson, charges that Hauerwas and other post-liberals have succumbed to what Gustafson calls "the sectarian temptation." As Christians acquire more and more ways of interpreting reality (through Freudian psychology, Marxist economic theory, genetics, and so on), the temptation grows for theologians to resist or reject nontheological means of interpreting events. Instead, these theologians simply assert the truth of traditional Christian beliefs, rather than revise them in light of discoveries in other fields. They attempt "to isolate Christian theology and ethics from critical external points of view in order to maintain the uniqueness or historic identity of Christianity."[30]

This strategy, Gustafson insists, exacts a heavy toll on the church. First, it asks Christians to ignore what the vast majority of them accept as credible methods of interpretation. Second, it minimizes the ability of Christians to engage in public discourse about matters of great moral importance. Third, it offers no guidelines to the church for knowing when its beliefs or practices should be altered.

Gustafson sees postliberals seeking to do the impossible when they commend, as George Lindbeck does, "the ancient practice of absorbing the universe into the biblical world."[31] It simply is no longer possible, argues Gustafson, to expect Christians to have "the Christian narrative" as the exclusive frame of interpretation for all events in their lives. As Gustafson explains in *An Examined Faith,*

> Everyone is exposed to multiple interpretations in daily papers and news magazines, in movies and on television—for example, *Nova*—and in other media. I know of few persons who use religious and theological symbols, concepts, and language as their first order of language to interpret themselves, their relationships, their health and illness, their work and leisure, or economic and political events, and so on, that occupy their attention.[32]

To ask Christians to ignore these alternative interpretations, Gustafson declares, "seems to me to create problems of moral and intellectual integrity for Christians; they would have to interpret and explain the same event in different ways as they left the doors of the Church and went home to read the newspapers, the scientific journals, or watch television."[33]

Gustafson also believes that by seeing Christian theology and Christian ethics as activities carried on by Christians for Christians, postliberals disengage from public moral debate. This posture prevents "Christianity from taking seriously the wider world of science and culture and limits the participation of Christians in the ambiguities of moral and social life in the patterns of interdependence in the world."[34]

Hauerwas has complained that this characterization of his position misses the mark. He insists that "the fact that I have doubts about the existence of any universal theory of justice does not mean that I think the church should avoid attempts to articulate concretely how this or that society should respond to the widow, the orphan, and the ill. What is needed, however, is not a theory of justice to secure that, but a people with the virtue of justice developed through the training of being part of a good community."[35] In other words, the church best informs the world of its ethical position on matters of ethical importance by first being the church and then by witnessing the gospel to the world.

Gustafson's third complaint is that Hauerwas and other postliberals provide no basis for assessing the beliefs and practices of the church. Gustafson writes,

> It is difficult to see how one can make any critique of the tradition, internal or external. Interestingly, I think Lindbeck does not give us a powerful doctrine of the revelation of God in the Scriptures; one is left with the impression that the task of doctrine is to maintain an aspect of culture called Christianity. This, in my terms, becomes sectarian, and also defensive. Doctrine

becomes ideology. It isolates theology from any correction by other modes of construing reality.[36]

Once preserving Christian identity becomes paramount, then the question of truth gets shortchanged. The theologian Terrence W. Tilley offers his assessment of this development: "Such theological moves are of real value, yet have profound weaknesses when the issue is not the evidence *of* or *in* the tradition, but the evidence *for* the tradition."[37]

When an element of the tradition is being called into question by a responsible critic who shares a commitment to many of the church's beliefs and practices, what role should extrabiblical arguments or claims play in that discussion? Hauerwas disputes Gustafson's claim that he and other postliberals isolate theology from correction from extrabiblical sources. Hauerwas insists, to the contrary, that he has not "tried to justify Christian belief by making Christian convictions immune from challenge from other modes of knowledge, particularly science."[38]

While Hauerwas insists that he has no interest in "making Christian conviction immune from challenge," his critics see little evidence of this in his writings. They point out that, while Hauerwas speaks of truth as an objective reality separate and apart from our perception, he does on occasion speak of truth as the reality created by the language we use. For example, critics are uneasy with Hauerwas's claim in *The Peaceable Kingdom* that "the narrative character of our knowledge of God, the self, and the world is a *reality-making claim* that the world and our existence in it are God's creation" [emphasis added].[39] Hauerwas's point is that our language shapes our very vision of the world. We construe reality; it is not an objective given, which many thinkers assume it to be.[40]

Demonstrating the truth of the Christian account of the world, Hauerwas continues, does not require that we offer a set of reasons that every person will accept but rather that Christians bear witness to that truth in the lives they lead. Christians must also remain open to the stranger. Hauerwas writes, "God comes to this community [i.e., the church] in the form of the stranger, challenging its smugness, exposing its temptations to false 'knowledge,' denying its spurious claims to have domesticated God's grace."[41] Many critics, however, do not see enough material evidence in Hauerwas's work of a commitment to correct the Christian tradition in light of developments in nontheological disciplines.[42]

The debate between Gustafson and the postliberals centers on the inevitable tension between two legitimate commitments: openness to change when the church is wrong and fidelity to the central teachings of the faith. The problem is knowing when which issue is at stake. Gustafson and other theologians who explicitly allow the findings from other areas of inquiry to alter Christians beliefs can point to the abolition of slavery as an example of when erroneous Christian moral teachings were overturned. In the field of science, the theory of evolution has altered how Christians read the creation stories in Genesis.

The postliberals, however, can point to the centrality of the resurrection as an example of a belief that Christians should never abandon, no matter how much the belief offends the cultural standard of reasonableness. For Hauerwas, pacifism is an essential, nonnegotiable feature of the Christian life. "Being a Christian and being a pacifist are not two things for me. I would not be a pacifist if I were not a Christian, and I find it hard to understand how one can be a Christian without being a pacifist."[43]

Hauerwas as a Postliberal Theologian

The emphasis on the particularity, rather than the universality, of Christian beliefs that we find in Hauerwas's work is a common theme among contemporary theological proponents of *postliberalism*. Classic theological liberals often grounded their theological claims in a general account of human experience (such as the experience of moral obligation or dependence on a greater power) and sought to demonstrate how Christian claims gave specific expression to this common human experience. Their aim was often to offer an account of Christian belief that conformed to the standards of rationality that were operative in the wider society.

Postliberals, in contrast, see all human experience as conditioned by the historical communities in which the experience takes place. Postliberals insist that Christianity is not a specific instance of the general human phenomenon of religion but a specific way of seeing the world that one acquires by being shaped by the language and practices of the Christian community. Debates regarding the reasonableness and intelligibility of Christian beliefs and practices are, as the late theologian Hans Frei insisted, "intramural" affairs that occur within specific communities. In this way, a belief or practice (such as Christian nonviolence) may make sense to Christians but strike those outside the Christian community as foolish or impractical.

The Future of Postliberal Theology

Postliberalism, as the very name suggests, is a movement that wants to challenge liberal political and theological assumptions in contemporary theology. In the standard postliberal account of the history of Christianity, the Enlightenment introduced theories of individualism and ahistorical reasoning that have proven detrimental to Christian thought and practice.

Thinkers such as Jeffrey Stout share many of Hauerwas's concerns about the present state of Christian thought, but they remain far more optimistic about liberal democratic institutions that developed throughout the modern age.[44] The debate between Hauerwas and Stout compels us to consider how Christians can best contribute to the greater common good of society and as such demonstrates the continued importance of postliberalism to contemporary Christian theology.

Conclusion

Hauerwas emphasizes the particularity of Christian convictions that are grounded in a specific narrative about the life, death, and resurrection of Jesus Christ. For John Cobb, whose theology is discussed in chapter 9, a more fitting image for contemporary Christian theology is the universality represented by the outpouring of the Holy Spirit on the crowd filled with people from different lands, speaking many different languages.

◉ Discussion Questions

1. Is it possible to construct an ethical theory that will be reasonable in the eyes of all rational people, or does every statement of ethics require a qualifier?

2. What *ethical* difference does the resurrection make in the lives of Christians?

3. Should Christians be pacifists? Why or why not?

4. In what sense does the world oppose Christian belief?

5. What does Hauerwas mean when he argues that the primary task of the church is to be the church? Do you agree or disagree with Hauerwas?

6. Does the church have the moral obligation to create a just society?

7. Should Christians revise their beliefs in light of scientific findings?

◎ Notes

1. Quoted in Colman McCarthy, "'America's Best Theologian' Walks Pacifist Road," *Free-Lance Star*, April 20, 2003. Available online at http://www.fredericksburg.com/News/FLS/2003/04 2003/04202003/944336/index_html.

2. Stanley Hauerwas, *The Peaceable Kingdom* (Notre Dame, Ind.: University of Notre Dame Press, 1983), p. 1.

3. Hauerwas, *The Peaceable Kingdom*, p. 100.

4. Ibid., p. 17.

5. Ibid., p. 62.

6. Ibid., p. 61.

7. Ibid., p. 22.

8. Ibid., p. 27.

9. Ibid., pp. 75–76.

10. Stanley Hauerwas, "Remembering John Howard Yoder: December 29, 1927–December 30, 1997," *First Things* 82 (1998): 15.

11. Stanley Hauerwas, "The Nonresistant Church: The Theological Ethics of John Howard Yoder," in *Vision and Virtue* (Notre Dame, Ind.: University of Notre Dame Press, 1981), p. 201.

12. Hauerwas, *The Peaceable Kingdom*, p. 76.

13. Stanley Hauerwas, "Jesus: The Story of the Kingdom," in *A Community of Character* (Notre Dame, Ind.: University of Notre Dame Press, 1981), p. 48.

14. Hauerwas, *The Peaceable Kingdom*, p. 76.

15. Stanley Hauerwas, "Should War Be Eliminated?" in *Against the Nations* (San Francisco: Harper & Row, 185), p. 205, n. 30. I discovered this quotation in Jeffrey S. Siker, *Scripture and Ethics* (New York: Oxford University Press, 1997), p. 103.

16. Hauerwas, *The Peaceable Kingdom*, p. 90.

17. Ibid., p. 79.

18. Ibid., p. 90.

19. Stanley Hauerwas, "On Not Holding On *or* Witnessing the Resurrection," in *Sanctify Them in the Truth* (Nashville, Tenn.: Abingdon Press, 1998), p. 261.

20. Hauerwas, *The Peaceable Kingdom*, pp. 88-89.

21. Ibid., p. 82.

22. Ibid., p. 99.

23 Hauerwas, *A Community of Character*, p. 50.

24. Stanley Hauerwas, "The Church in a Divided World: The Interpretative Power of the Christian Story," in *A Community of Character* (Notre Dame, Ind.: University of Notre Dame Press, 1981), p. 109.

25. Hauerwas, *The Peaceable Kingdom*, p. 104.

26. Ibid., p. 106.

27. I owe this point to an unpublished paper by Joseph Incandela.

28. Hauerwas, *The Peaceable Kingdom*, p. 105.

29. Ibid., p. 100.

30. James M. Gustafson, "The Sectarian Temptation: Reflections on Theology, the Church, and the University," *Proceedings of the Catholic Theological Society* 40 (1985): 83.

31. The Lindbeck quote appears in his work *The Nature of Doctrine* (Philadelphia: Westminster Press, 1984), p. 135. Gustafson cites the sentence in "The Sectarian Temptation," p. 86; *An Examined Faith* (Minneapolis: Fortress Press, 2004); and "Just What is 'Postliberal' Theology?" *Christian Century*, March 24–31, 1999, p. 354.

32. Gustafson, *An Examined Faith*, p. 8.

33. Gustafson, "The Sectarian Temptation," p. 91. The postliberal William Placher replies to Gustafson on this point in "Being Postliberal: A Response to James Gustafson," *Christian Century*, April 7, 1999, p. 391.

34. Gustafson, "The Sectarian Temptation," p. 84.

35. Stanley Hauerwas, "Will the Real Sectarian Stand Up?" *Theology Today* 44, no. 1 (1987): 89.

36. Gustafson, "The Sectarian Temptation," p. 86.

37. Terrence W. Tilley, *History, Theology, and Faith* (Maryknoll, N.Y.: Orbis Books, 2004), p. 2.

38. Stanley Hauerwas, "Introduction," in *Christian Existence Today* (Durham, N.C.: Labyrinth Press, 1988), p. 9. This introduction is Hauerwas's rebuttal to Gustafson's "The Sectarian Temptation."

39. Hauerwas, *The Peaceable Kingdom*, p. 25. Emphasis added.

40. For an illustration of this theme, see Hauerwas's discussion of the Nuer people in *The Peaceable Kingdom*, pp. 116–117.

41. Hauerwas, *Christian Existence Today*, p. 11.

42. For a critique of Hauerwas along these lines, see William J. Meyer, "On Keeping Theological Ethics Theological: An

Alternative to Hauerwas's Diagnosis and Prescription," *Annual of the Society of Christian Ethics* 19 (1999): 21–45. It is also interesting in this regard to note Richard Hays's claim in *The Moral Vision of the New Testament* (San Francisco: Harper & Row, 1996) that in recent years Hauerwas has moved into "an aggressively postmodern phase, denying that texts, including the Bible, have meaning save as they are construed within particular interpretive communities" (p. 254).

43. Stanley Hauerwas, "September 11, 2001: A Pacifist Response," in *Performing the Faith* (Grand Rapids, Mich.: Brazos Press, 2004), p. 201.

44. See Jeffrey Stout, *Democracy and Tradition* (Princeton, N.J.: Princeton University Press, 2004). See also Hauerwas's "Postscript" to *Performing the Faith* (Grand Rapids, Mich.: Brazos Press, 2004).

⊚ Suggested Readings

For an anthology of Hauerwas's writings, see John Berkman and Michael Cartwright, *The Hauerwas Reader* (Durham, N.C.: Duke University Press, 2001).

For an introduction to Hauerwas's work, see Samuel Wells, *Transforming Fate into Destiny* (Eugene, Ore.: Cascade Books, 1998).

Hauerwas's Gifford Lectures were published as *With the Grain of the Universe* (Grand Rapids, Mich.: Brazos, 2001).

Helpful summaries of Hauerwas's work can be found in Jeffrey S. Siker, *Scripture and Ethics* (New York: Oxford University Press, 1997), and R. Scott Smith, *Virtue Ethics and Moral Knowledge* (Burlington, Vt.: Ashgate, 2003).

For a critical engagement with Hauerwas's views on liberal democracy, see Jeffrey Stout, *Democracy and Tradition* (Princeton, N.J.: Princeton University Press, 2004).

Chapter 9

Pentecost: John Cobb Jr. and Pluralism

How does Christianity relate to other religions?

✎ *Looking Ahead*

John Cobb (1925–) is an ordained Methodist minister whose work draws from philosophical analysis and is described as representing pluralism. Pluralism in theology means that Christianity can assimilate, or take on, insights from other sources, including other world religions, while still retaining the truth of Christian belief and doctrine. For Cobb, theological questions remain open to new understandings as the process of living an authentic life unfolds. Note especially how Cobb points to ways in which Christ affects the contemporary world.

In the first chapter of Acts of the Apostles, Christ ascends to heaven after telling the apostles to remain in Jerusalem to await the fulfillment of "the promise of the Father. "'This,' he said, 'is what you have heard from me; for John baptized with water, but you will be baptized with the Holy Spirit not many days from now'" (1:4–5). This promise is fulfilled in dramatic fashion at Pentecost. Originally a harvest festival in Judaism, Pentecost becomes in Christian thought the occasion on which the apostles were given the gift of the Holy Spirit, empowering them to carry the good news to the ends of the earth.

Pentecost, with its emphasis on the dynamic and pervasive influence of God throughout every culture on Earth, is a fitting symbol for the work of John Cobb (1925–), a leading proponent of a movement in contemporary thought known as *process theology*. Central to Cobb's work is the question, How does Christianity relate to other religions?

Biography of John Cobb

In many ways, the circumstances of John Cobb's childhood anticipated his life-long academic interests. He was born in Japan, where his parents were Christian missionaries. He remained with them there until the outbreak of World War II, at which time he moved to the United States to live with his grandmother.[1] At age eighteen, he volunteered for service in the U.S. Army.

While stationed at Camp Ritchie in Maryland, Cobb felt called to the ministry. "I was walking to a Presbyterian church a couple of miles from camp, just across the state boundary in Pennsylvania. . . . Suddenly, I stopped. Out of the blue, it seemed, it had come to me that I should be a minister."[2] Cobb would eventually become an ordained minister in the United Methodist Church. It was also in the intelligence division of the army that Cobb worked beside Catholic and Jewish intellectuals. He writes, "Through contact with them, I came for the first time to recognize that my southern Methodist piety was only one, quite peculiar, form of religious life, and that indeed Christian faith in general was a highly questionable matter from many points of view."[3]

When Cobb left the army in 1946, he enrolled at the University of Chicago, where he earned his doctorate in 1952. During his studies there, Cobb experienced a crisis of faith as he immersed himself in the study of the criticisms of Christianity.

Because it was the modern worldview in general that was the obstacle to Christian faith, the thinking that helped me most was that which focused on transcending it. My need was to find a worldview that took seriously what had been accomplished by modernity, but went beyond it. I found that in the cosmology of Whitehead. It was through that discovery that I was able, slowly and painfully, to reconstruct for myself a Christian vision.[4]

Cobb found the foundation for an alternative understanding of Christianity, which he would develop throughout the course of his academic and pastoral career, in the process philosophy of Alfred North Whitehead, a nineteenth- and twentieth-century mathematician, logician, and philosopher. Whitehead's views were first brought to the University of Chicago in 1927 by the theologian Henry Nelson Wieman,[5] and Cobb's own graduate studies at Chicago were directed by Charles Hartshorne,[6] another pioneering figure in the field of process thought.

The bulk of Cobb's professional career was spent at Claremont, where he also established the influential Center for Process Studies. His wide range of interests have included interreligious dialogue, ecological issues, and economics. He retired in 1990.

God in Process Theology

Alfred North Whitehead challenged the dominant Western theological belief that God exists outside time. Classical theology reasoned that because God is a perfect being, God cannot change. Change would mean that God either lacked some perfection earlier or lost some perfection later. Neither of these changes, the argument continues, would befit a perfect being. As the religious philosopher C. Stephen Evans explains, "Obviously a perfect being must possess a degree of stability; one would not want to worship a God who radically altered his character on a whim.

Classically, many theists, especially those who think of God as timelessly eternal, have believed that God is absolutely unchangeable or *immutable*."[7]

By contrast, Whitehead and today's process theologians believe that God is necessarily affected by human suffering. The late theologian John Macquarrie poignantly expressed the issue as follows:

> The traditional belief is that God is active, but not passive, that he affects the world but it not affected by it. But what kind of God would that be? A God without *pathos*, an apathetic God, which is indeed a literal translation of the expression which some of the Greek fathers used about God. Such a God could not be a God of love, for to love is to be vulnerable and to lay oneself open to suffering. If God is supremely love, must he not also be supremely touched by suffering, grieved by the countless pains of all the creatures whom he loves? Indeed, could we rightly apply the name "God" if God were totally untouched by suffering?[8]

Process theologians insist that Whitehead's understanding of God aligns with the message of the Old Testament prophets, especially Hosea, who spoke of both God's anger and tenderness.

Process theologians therefore propose that we conceive of God as having two poles, aspects, or natures. The first is God's *primordial nature,* and the second is God's *consequent nature.* Just as the human mind and body are distinct yet interrelated aspects of the human person, so, too, does God have both mental (primordial) and physical (consequent) aspects. The primordial nature is the storehouse of possibilities or aims that are offered to humanity. In their freedom, humans can choose to actualize these possibilities or reject them. These decisions and events then become part of the consequent nature of God. This ongoing, dynamic process—in which the possible becomes the actual, which in turn creates a new range of possibilities for actualization in the succession of moments that follow—is part of the very nature of God.

Process theologians believe that Whitehead's scheme presents a more holistic understanding of the relationship between God and the world. In *God and the World*, Cobb writes,

> God's standpoint is all-inclusive, and so, in a sense we are parts of God. But we are not parts of God in the sense that God is simply the sum total of the parts or that the parts are lacking in independence and self-determination. God and the creatures interact as separate entities, while God includes the standpoints of all of them in his omnispatial standpoint. In this sense God is everywhere, but he is not everything. The world does not exist outside God or apart from God, but the world is not God or simply part of God. The character of the world is influenced by God, but it is not determined by him, and the world in its turn contributes novelty and richness to the divine experience.[9]

Not only does this account of the God-world relationship have profound implications for issues of ecology, but it also presents a framework for understanding how God took on human flesh and dwelt among us. Cobb's own extended exploration of that issue appeared in 1975 with the publication of *Christ in a Pluralistic Age*.[10]

Cobb's *Christ in a Pluralistic Age*

The ancient concept of the *Logos* is at the heart of Cobb's very modern christology. Christians are most familiar with the appearance of the word *Logos* in the prologue of John's gospel: "In the beginning was the Word [*Logos*], and the Word was with God, and the Word was God" (1:1).

Christians, of course, believe that "the Word became flesh and lived among us" (John 1:14) in the person of Jesus Christ.

While the incarnation of the Word is for all Christians the preeminent expression of the Word, thinkers in the early church did not regard the incarnation as the only manifestation of the Logos in human history. For example, the theologian Donald K. McKim discusses the role of the Logos in the theology of the second-century Christian thinker Justin Martyr:

> He adopts the Greek concept of the *logos* (thought, word, reason) as a way to explain how the great gulf between God and humanity was bridged. In accord with Greek thought, Justin says that humans are united with God by reason and know God through reason. Prior to the coming of Christ, humans had "seeds of the Logos" (*logos spermatikos*) and could thus gain fragmentary truths about God. These were actually "Christians before Christ." . . . The function of the Logos is to be the Father's agent, creating and ordering the universe, and to reveal truth to humanity.[11]

In *Beyond Dialogue,* Cobb also refers to the contribution Justin Martyr made to Christian thought: "Justin Martyr viewed the gods of the pagans as demons, but as he confronted Greek philosophy he found much that he admired and adopted. This affinity he attributed to the work of the Logos. . . . Thus while Christ stands against idolatry and worship of demons, Christ is the fulfillment of the fragmentary truth that is present in the world of Gentile thought."[12]

The belief that Jesus of Nazareth was the Incarnate Word (*Logos*) of God provided the backdrop for many early church controversies regarding the nature of Christ and the Trinity. The first question to arise centered on the precise relationship between the Word and God. If Jesus, who walked on this earth, was the Incarnate Word and he prayed to the Father in heaven, does this mean that there are two Gods? The church tackled this question of Christ's divinity at the Council of Nicaea in 325 and declared that Christ was "of the same substance" or "one in being with" the Father.[13] Only God can give us eternal life. Christ gives eternal life. Therefore, Christ is divine. The second question followed logically from the first: How can divinity and humanity coexist in one person? After various solutions were offered, the bishops declared at the Council of Chalcedon in 451 that Christ was one person in two natures. They are "together the one and only and only-begotten Logos of God, the Lord Jesus Christ."[14] The decrees of the Councils of Nicaea and Chalcedon remain the benchmark of an orthodox christology.

Christ in a Pluralistic Age

In the introduction to *Christ in a Pluralistic Age,* Cobb makes this declaration: "Can Christ be alive when his image has passed from our basic vision? This book is an affirmative answer to that question."[15]

After making this declaration, Cobb develops an extended defense of the relevance of Christ (as understood through the categories of process thought) for the modern world. Such a proposal, writes Cobb, requires that we deal with two unavoidable elements of modern thought: "the profane consciousness" and "pluralism."[16] The *profane consciousness* relies on the traditional distinction between sacred and the profane (the holy and the ordinary). The profane consciousness sees Christ as confined to religious matters and increasingly interprets the world in purely secular terms. The latter element, *pluralism,* develops as we achieve greater and greater awareness of the world's radically different religious traditions. This recognition prompts Christians (1) to reject the truth of other religions, (2) to assume naively that all religions are describing the same experience in different language, or (3) to drop all references to "Christ" and speak instead in generalities, such as "the ultimate" or "the divine spirit."[17] Cobb seeks to offer a worldview that does not oppose the sacred and the profane, instead seeing both as an integrated whole, and to preserve a commitment to Christ while allowing for Christianity to assimilate the truth of other religions.

Cobb believes that the unique challenges of modern thought can be best addressed when we see Christ as "the image of creative transformation." Cobb writes, "Christ, as the image of creative transformation, can provide a unity within which the many centers of meaning and existence can be appreciated and encouraged and through which openness to the other great Ways of mankind can lead to a deepening of Christian experience."[18] Rather than accept the profane consciousness, which sees a limited role for Christ in the world, creative transformation encompasses a wide range of social, political, and cultural forces of change. Rather than see pluralism as an insurmountable problem, creative transformation acknowledges the relativity of all perspectives without succumbing to the belief that truth itself is relative. Such affirmations can be made, Cobb continues, if we see human existence as constantly enriched by novel possibilities that form and reform our understanding of reality.

The image of Christ as creative transformation functions in Cobb's theology as the equivalent of the traditional Christian claim that Christ is the Incarnate *Logos*.

> In the Christian tradition the transcendent reality that in its incarnate form is named Christ is called the Logos. Christ is the Logos as incarnate. The Logos is the cosmic principle of order, the ground of meaning, and the source of purpose. Whitehead has called this

transcendent source of the aim at the new the principle of concretion, the principle of limitation, the organ of novelty, the lure for feeling, the eternal urge of desire, the divine Eros, and God in his Primordial Nature.[19]

In traditional theological language, the Logos is both a transcendent and an immanent reality. "The Logos in its transcendence is timeless and infinite, but in its incarnation or immanence it is always a specific force for just that creative transformation which is possible and optimal in each situation."[20] Because the Logos is immanently present in all events in human history, Christians see Christ at work in all aspects of human existence. "The implication of this analysis is that God as Logos is effectively, if unconsciously, present and felt in all events. The Logos is truly incarnate in the world. Christ is a reality in the world."[21]

The Logos has both a stabilizing and destabilizing role in human history. It functions as "a transcendent ground of order"[22] that preserves each moment as it passes from the present into the past. The other function of the Logos is "to introduce tension between what has been and what might be and continuously to challenge and upset the established order for the sake of the new."[23] This combination of continuity with the past and openness to the future provides the conditions for vitality, creativity, and growth. As Cobb and David Griffin explain,

Creative transformation is the essence of growth, and growth is the essence of life. Growth is not achieved by merely adding together elements in the given world in different combinations. It requires the transformation of those elements through the introduction of novelty. It alters their nature and meaning without suppressing or destroying them. The source of the novelty is the Logos, whose incarnation is Christ. Where Christ is effectively present, there is creative transformation.[24]

This element of novelty that the Logos continuously introduces is central to the vision of the world presented by process theology.[25]

In part 2 of *Christ in a Pluralistic Age,* Cobb turns his attention to the relationship between the Logos and the actual Jesus of Nazareth. Cobb writes, "Among other ways Jesus has affected history, two are selected for special attention in this part: his message and his objective efficacy."[26] Cobb sifts through the historical findings of four scholars with a wide range of beliefs (Rudolf Bultmann, Norman Perrin, Ernest Cadman Colwell, and Milan Machovec) to construct an account of the message preached by Jesus of Nazareth that would, in Cobb's view, be widely accepted by historians examining the gospels.

The parable of the Pharisee and the tax collector (Luke 18:9–14) captures for Cobb an essential feature of the message of Jesus: "the reversal of expectation and the consequent crisis."[27] By praising the contrite public sinner, rather than the complacent religious leader, Jesus challenges the socially accepted norms of holiness of his listeners. By the "objective efficacy" of Jesus, Cobb means the traditional Christian claim that in Jesus we find salvation, or "the positive new reality into which, through the transformation of the old, we are introduced."[28]

For Cobb, this reality is nicely described by Paul in the passages that speak of Christians as living in Christ (2 Corinthians 5:17) or as having been clothed with Christ (Galatians 3:27). Cobb writes, "Since Christ was distinctively related to God, to be in Christ is to be conformed in some measure to that relationship, hence through Christ one shares in grace, peace, and joy with God. Through the conformation, the righteousness of Christ becomes our righteousness."[29]

Cobb attaches great significance to the authority with which Jesus proclaimed his message. For Cobb, this suggests that Jesus had a "structure of existence" that was a unique instance in human history—a life of a fully human person giving an unqualified acceptance to the Logos at each moment in time. "The Logos is incarnate in all human beings and indeed in all creation, but it does not provide all with the certainty of God's will or the authority of direct insight,"[30] writes Cobb. Jesus, like all human beings, had the presence of the Logos within him. Cobb speculates, however, that while most humans resist the prompting of the Logos or often perceive it as a threat to the self, Jesus fully embraced the Logos at each moment of his existence. Such an explanation would account for the authority with which Jesus spoke and would support the traditional affirmation proclaimed at the Council of Chalcedon that Jesus was one person in two natures. "Jesus, without in any way ceasing to be human, participated in that one structure of existence in which the self is coconstituted by the presence of God."[31]

In part 3 of *Christ in a Pluralistic Age,* Cobb addresses the images of hope generated by Jesus Christ within the Christian tradition. He highlights four images drawn from the Christian tradition and describes their relevance for contemporary theology. First, the image of "the City of God," most commonly associated with St. Augustine (354–430), becomes, in Cobb's usage, an image for modern urban planning. Second, "the Perfection of Love" deals with the fruits of Christianity's encounter with Buddhism. Third, Cobb correlates "the Kingdom of Heaven" with Whitehead's concept of the consequent nature of God that preserves the past. Fourth, the "Resurrection of the Dead" focuses on the issue of Jesus' resurrection and, by extension, the issue of personal immortality.

All four images relate to a dimension of the hope that we find in Christ. The creative transformation that fuels this hope is both present and future (City of God), Western and Eastern (Perfection of Love), temporal and eternal

(Kingdom of Heaven), and personal and social (Resurrection of the Dead). All four images also express the creative transformation that is possible when we enter into what Cobb calls "the field of force generated by Jesus."[32]

> The openness to creative transformation that is faith in relation to the present can be sustained only in the context of hope, but the hope and the images of hope are themselves expressions of creative transformation. Both the openness and the hope require that we be renewed in our openness by the support of a community that expresses the field of force generated by Jesus and that is renewed by encounter with his words. Jesus opens us to the present working of the Logos by assuring us of our future. Hope enables us to hear the words of Jesus and to conform to him.[33]

The ground of hope is Christ, the Christian designation of the Logos at work in human history.

The Perfection of Love model illustrates Cobb's long-standing interest in Buddhist-Christian dialogue. While Cobb suggests that "Christianity can be creatively transformed through interiorization of this alien tradition,"[34] he insists that this dialogue needs to take the proper form. In his essay "Beyond 'Pluralism,'" Cobb rejects two strategies for interreligious dialogue. The first strategy is to claim that all religions essentially teach the same principles. Cobb finds fault with the assumption that there is either a common definition of *religion* or a common essence to all religions. The second strategy that Cobb rejects endorses a conceptual relativism that reduces all religious claims as truth for those who accept that religion, rather than for all people. The notion of conceptual relativism "seems to do justice to each tradition, but in fact it vitiates the claims of all, since all claim at least some elements of universality."[35]

What form, then, should interreligious dialogue take? Cobb writes, "One enters dialogue both as a believer convinced of the claims of one religious tradition and as a human being open to the possibility that one has something to learn from representatives of another religious tradition."[36] Dialogue does not require that we surrender our deepest convictions about reality, but it does require that both parties remain open to mutual transformation.[37] This is not merely a matter of Buddhism integrating the truths of Christianity but also of Christianity integrating the truths of Buddhism.

The belief that the Logos operates in all human persons provides the basis for genuine interreligious dialogue. Truth extends beyond the Christian tradition. "The belief that there is more to truth and wisdom than one's own tradition has thus far attained is the basis for overcoming the alternatives of essentialism and conceptual relativism. It entails the belief that while one's own tradition has grasped important aspects of reality, reality in its entirety is always more."[38]

Assessments of Cobb's *Christ in a Pluralistic Age*

Cobb's christological proposals in *Christ in a Pluralistic Age* have, of course, not gone unchallenged. In a review of Cobb's work, the theologian Gabriel Fackre expresses reservations regarding Cobb's treatment of the uniqueness of Jesus. Cobb's discussion centers on the universal working of the Logos, not on the particular person, Jesus of Nazareth. Fackre warns that "a question must be raised here about the identification of the incarnate Logos with the universal working of a metaphysical process rather than the radical particularity of one physical event."[39] Fackre would be concerned with Cobb's statement that the "Logos is incarnate in all human beings."[40]

In what sense, then, is Jesus unique? Cobb's answer is that we can best describe Jesus' uniqueness in terms of the degree to which he allowed his personal identity to be shaped by the Logos. Fackre finds such an answer insufficient.

> While it may be vociferously argued that the difference in degree is so astronomical that it amounts to a difference in kind, or that unity of self and Logos is so intense that there is a unique coalescence, these assertions miss the point of the classical insistence on once-happenedness. The singularity of Jesus is bound up with the conviction that something cosmic had been *done* in Christ that finally rid the world of its perennial foes. The exemplification of a quality or process that is universal is too static and conservative a view of this revolutionary event.[41]

In Fackre's estimation, Cobb's christology does not adequately capture the decisiveness with which Jesus' death and resurrection defeated the power of sin and death.

Other critics have raised concerns about process theology's general account of God's power and, more specifically, the ability of God to act decisively in human history. The philosopher James A. Keller summarizes the position of process theologians as follows:

> Process theists typically assert that their understanding of the power of God enables them to solve the problem of evil more satisfactorily than classical theists can, given their understanding of God's power. They claim that according to classical theism, God has the power to intervene decisively at any time and place to bring about any logically possible outcome that God wants; thus, classical theists must admit that God at least permits whatever evils occur. By contrast, process theists

deny that God has such power; thus, they do not have to admit that God even permits the evils that occur.[42]

Process theologians assert that God acts persuasively, not coercively, in human affairs. As Cobb states, "If we are to think of God as exercising any significant power upon our lives, we must think—as surely the New Testament thinks—of the kind of power exercised by a wise and effective parent and not that of a potter."[43]

Critics maintain that process theologians' understanding of God's power fails to account for unilateral acts of God in creation *ex nihilo* (out of nothing), Christ's resurrection, and the eschatological establishment of the Kingdom of God. Cobb and Griffin assert, for example, that process theology "does insist that the future is truly open and that what will happen depends upon what human beings will do."[44] Process theologians argue that their theology allows for genuine human free will. If humans would act so irresponsibly as to cause the destruction of the human race, then God could not act unilaterally to prevent that catastrophe from occurring. Cobb and Griffin conclude, "God persuades against it, but there is no guarantee that we will give heed. Goes does not act *ex machina* to prevent the consequences of destructive human acts."[45]

The Future of Pluralism

The threat of pluralism is *relativism*. Given the dizzying array of views about the nature of the divine, the meaning of life, and moral truth, how can we possibly ever know who is right? Perhaps there is no one universal right answer. Perhaps there is only an answer that is right for each individual.

In certain aspects of life, this may well be true, but if there is no right answer to *any* question, then we confront the problem of relativism. If the individual becomes the arbiter of what is real and one person's reality is as equally valid as the next person's, then moral discourse is meaningless and religious and philosophical debate is merely recreational.

The picture here is a bleak one, but that alone does not mean that it is inaccurate. The task of the theologian is to demonstrate, in some way, that the picture is wrong. Therefore, the pluralism that we encounter increasingly invests questions of truth, certainty, and meaningfulness with an even greater urgency. Contemporary Christian theology faces the challenge of embracing diversity and plurality of thought while also upholding moral truth in a world too often torn by violence.

Conclusion

Cobb's process theology requires that we consider both the future and the ultimate end of human history. It is to that final moment in the Christian narrative that we next turn our attention. In the next chapter, we will discuss the relation between how we view the future and how we live in the present, as found in the theology of Wolfhart Pannenberg.

⊛ Discussion Questions

1. What, in your view, is the importance of Pentecost for Christian belief and action?

2. Whitehead once described God as "the great companion, the fellow-sufferer who understands." What is your evaluation of this statement? Is a suffering God a positive or negative image for you?

3. Is the Logos at work in human history? Is the Logos present in each human person? What are the implications of your answer for how we understand current social and political movements?

4. What does Cobb mean when he labels Christ as "creative transformation"? Do you agree or disagree with Cobb's claim?

5. What should be the Christian stance toward other religions? How does this relate to the scriptural assertion that Jesus is "the way, and the truth, and the life" (John 14:6)?

6. Does God have the power to act unilaterally in human history? Does human free will limit God's power in any way?

7. What is your overall assessment of process theology? What advantages and disadvantages does it have, compared to other theologies discussed in this book, for empowering Christians to live an authentic life?

Notes

1. For biographical information, I am relying on these sources: Marjorie Hewitt Suchocki, "John B. Cobb, Jr." in Donald W. Musser and Joseph L. Price, eds., *A New Handbook of Christian Theologians* (Nashville, Tenn.: Abingdon Press, 1996); Ed. L. Miller and Stanley Grenz, *Fortress Introduction to Contemporary Theologies* (Minneapolis: Fortress Press, 1998), chapter 7; David Ray Griffin, "John B. Cobb, Jr.: A Theological Biography," in David Ray Griffin and Joseph C. Hough, Jr., eds., *Theology and the University* (Albany: State University of New York Press, 1991), appendix A; and two of Cobb's autobiographical essays: "Christ and My Life," in *Can Christ Become Good News Again?* (St. Louis: Chalice Press, 1991), chapter 1, and "Intellectual Autobiography," *Religious Studies Review* 19, no. 1 (1995).

2. Cobb, "Christ and My Life," p. 6.

3. Ibid., p. 8.

4. Cobb, "Intellectual Autobiography," p. 9.

5. Griffin, "John B. Cobb, Jr.: A Theological Biography," p. 229.

6. Suchocki, "John B. Cobb, Jr.," p. 106.

7. C. Stephen Evans, *Philosophy of Religion* (Downers Grove, Ill.: InterVarsity Press, 1985), p. 36. Emphasis in original.

8. John Macquarrie, *In Search of Deity* (New York: Crossroad, 1984), p. 41. Emphasis in original.

9. John B. Cobb Jr., *God and the World* (Philadelphia: Westminster Press, 1969), pp. 79–80.

10. John B. Cobb Jr., *Christ in a Pluralistic Age* (Philadelphia: Westminster Press, 1975).

11. Donald K. McKim, *Theological Turning Points* (Atlanta: John Knox Press, 1988), p. 9.

12. John B. Cobb Jr., *Beyond Dialogue* (Philadelphia: Fortress Press, 1982), p. 5.

13. See R.A. Norris, "Homoousios," in Alan Richardson and John Bowden, eds. *The Westminster Dictionary of Christian Theology* (Philadelphia: Westminster Press, 1983), p. 270.

14. "The Definition of Chalcedon," in John H. Leith, ed., *Creeds of the Churches*, 3rd ed. (Atlanta: John Knox Press, 1982), p. 36.

15. Cobb, *Christ in a Pluralistic Age*, p. 17.

16. Ibid., p. 18.

17. Ibid., p. 20.

18. Ibid., p. 21.

19. Ibid., p. 71.

20. Ibid., p. 72.

21. Ibid., p. 77.

22. Ibid., p. 75.

23. Ibid., p. 84.

24. John B. Cobb Jr. and David Ray Griffin, *Process Theology: An Introductory Exposition* (Philadelphia: Westminster Press, 1976), p. 100.

25. Cobb and Griffin, *Process Theology*, p. 28.

26. Cobb, *Christ in a Pluralistic Age*, p. 99.

27. Ibid., p. 110.

28. Ibid., p. 111.

29. Ibid., p. 122.

30. Ibid., p. 138.

31. Ibid., p. 171.

32. Ibid., p. 185.

33. Ibid.

34. Ibid., p. 205.

35. John B. Cobb Jr., "Beyond 'Pluralism,'" in Gavin D'Costa, ed., *Christian Uniqueness Reconsidered* (Maryknoll, N.Y.: Orbis Books, 1990), p. 85.

36. Cobb, "Beyond 'Pluralism,'" pp. 85–86.
37. See Cobb, *Beyond Dialogue*, p. 48.
38. Cobb, "Beyond 'Pluralism,'" p. 86.
39. Gabriel Fackre, "Cobb's *Christ in a Pluralistic Age*: A Review Article," *Andover Newton Quarterly* 17, no. 4 (1977): 312. I would like to thank Diana Yount in the Archives and Special Collections office at Andover Newton Theological School for her invaluable assistance in locating this review for me.
40. Cobb, *Christ in a Pluralistic Age*, p. 138.
41. Fackre, "Cobb's *Christ*," p. 314. Emphasis in original. See also Jerry K. Robbins, "A Reader's Guide to Process Christology," *Encounter* 53, no. 1 (1992): 88.
42. James A. Keller, "The Power of God and Miracles in Process Theism," *Journal of the American Academy of Religion* 63, no. 1 (1995): 105.
43. Cobb, *God and the World*, p. 90.
44. Cobb and Griffin, *Process Theology*, p. 118.
45. Ibid., p. 118.

◎ Suggested Readings

For an introduction to Cobb's theology, see chapter 7 of Ed. L. Miller and Stanley Grenz, *Fortress Introduction to Contemporary Theologies* (Minneapolis: Fortress Press, 1998). Another helpful resource is Ted Peters, "John Cobb: Theologian in Process," in two parts in *Dialog* 29 (1990): 207–220 and *Dialog* 30 (1991): 290–302.

For an introduction to the leading thinkers in process theology, see chapter 10 of James C. Livingston and Francis Schüssler Fiorenza, *Modern Christian Thought*, 2nd ed., vol. 2 (Minneapolis: Fortress Press, 2006). For another introductory text, see John B. Cobb Jr. and David Ray Griffin, *Process Theology: An Introductory Exposition* (Philadelphia: Westminster Press, 1976).

For a glossary of process theology terms, see Marjorie Hewitt Suchocki, *God, Christ, Church*, rev. ed. (New York: Crossroad Press, 1989), pp. 257–259.

For a more difficult yet very helpful analysis of Cobb's christology, see Wolfhart Pannenberg, "A Liberal Logos Christology:

The Christology of John Cobb," in David Ray Griffin and Thomas
J. J. Altizer, eds., *John Cobb's Theology in Process* (Philadelphia:
Westminster Press, 1977).

For Cobb's own reflections on christology in the decade following
publication of *Christ in a Pluralistic Age,* as well as critical remarks
by fellow scholars, see John B. Cobb Jr., "Christ Beyond Creative
Transformation," in Stephen T. Davis, ed., *Encountering Jesus*
(Atlanta: John Knox Press, 1988).

Chapter 10

The End of Time: Wolfhart Pannenberg and Hermeneutical Theology

Is there a final goal for human history?

> ✎ *Looking Ahead*
>
> Wolfhart Pannenberg (1928–), a Protestant theologian, was baptized Lutheran and represents what is termed hermeneutical theology. Hermeneutics, strictly 'the science of interpretation,' refers to the way of reading and interpreting ancient texts for contemporary audiences. Look especially for Pannenberg's insights into eschatology, or the study of the end of the world, and the questions it raises for contemporary Christian living.

Wolfhart Pannenberg's theology can be seen as a counterproposal to much of what had become the norm in twentieth-century German theology. Pannenberg brings to his theology a confidence in human beings' ability to recognize God's revelation, in history's ability to display that revelation, and in Scripture's ability to preserve that revelation. Pannenberg resists the tendency on the part of many theologians to insist that faith is a necessary component for recognizing the revelation of God. By contrast, as Stanley J. Grenz and Roger E. Olson explain,

[Pannenberg] sees theology as a public discipline related to the quest for universal truth. For him the truth question is to be answered in the process of theological reflection and reconstruction. He criticizes any attempt to divide truth into autonomous spheres or to shield the truth content of the Christian tradition from rational inquiry. Theological affirmations must be subjected to the rigor of critical inquiry concerning the historical reality on which they are based. Theology, in other words, must be evaluated on the basis of critical canons, just as other sciences, for it also deals with truth.[1]

Pannenberg also repeatedly insists that God's revelation does not exist in a realm of eternity separate and distinct from the flow of history or in the recesses of the human heart apart from public view. Instead, God's revelation is historical. Pannenberg speaks of the "indirect self-revelation of God through the history in which God is active."[2]

In addition, Pannenberg rejects the claims of those who argue that the Scriptures are hopelessly compromised as historical sources. Although he certainly employs the tools of modern biblical scholarship, he does not believe that this necessitates a wholesale discounting of the historical reliability of the scriptural stories. Pannenberg argues for the historic accuracy of the resurrection stories of the empty tomb (which, he argues, could easily have been disproven if they were false) and the tradition of the appearances of the resurrected Lord.

The significance of the resurrection, contends Pannenberg, is twofold: First, it sheds light on the pre-Easter career of Jesus, and second, it anticipates the future. In terms of its meaning for the pre-Easter career of Jesus, James C. Livingston and Francis Schüssler Fiorenza explain, "Pannenberg also asserts the retroactivity of the resurrection in a creative attempt to take into account the full humanity of Jesus and those New Testament verses that speak of Jesus's inauguration as Son of God at his resurrection. Pannenberg asserts that although Jesus is appointed the Son of God at his resurrection, he is retroactively the Son of God from the beginning of his life."[3] In other words, Pannenberg argues from the resurrection to the incarnation.

Our present investigation, however, requires that we follow Pannenberg's second line of argumentation that is proleptic or anticipatory in nature. Livingston and Fiorenza continue, "What Pannenberg means by the proleptic and anticipatory nature of the resurrection is that the end of history is already anticipated and realized in the event of Jesus' resurrection."[4] It is this second meaning, this proleptic or anticipatory meaning, that will occupy our attention in this chapter as we pursue the question, Is there a final goal for human history?

Biography of Wolfhart Pannenberg

Wolfhart Pannenberg was born in Stettin, in northern Germany (now part of Poland) in 1928, and although baptized into the Lutheran church, he did not have a religious upbringing. An experience at age sixteen, however, helped to convince him of God's existence.

> The single most important experience occurred in early January 1945, when I was 16 years old. On a lonely two-hour walk home from my piano lesson, seeing an otherwise ordinary sunset. I was suddenly flooded by light and absorbed in a sea of light, which, although it did not extinguish the humble awareness of my finite experience, overflowed the barriers that normally separate us from the surrounding world. Several months earlier I had narrowly escaped an American bombardment at Berlin; a few weeks later my family would have to leave our East German home because of the Russian offensive. I did not know at the time that January 6 was the day of Epiphany, nor did I realize that in that moment

Jesus Christ claimed my life as a witness to the transfiguration of this world in the illuminating power and judgment of his glory. But there began a period of craving to understand the meaning of the life, and since philosophy did not seem to offer the ultimate answers to such a quest, I finally decided to probe the Christian tradition more seriously than I had considered worthwhile before.[5]

Pannenberg initially intended to pursue a career in philosophy, but later, while a student in Berlin, he became impressed with the thinking of the theologian Karl Barth. By the time Pannenberg completed his doctoral studies at Heidelberg, he had combined his philosophical and theological interests. In his theology, Pannenberg attempts to offer a rationally defensible position regarding the central claims of Christianity (for example, Christ's resurrection) in light of the historical evidence available. Pannenberg has spent most of his academic career (1968–1993) at the University of Munich.[6]

Our investigation of Pannenberg's own thinking will comprise three parts. First, we will situate his discussion of the proleptic or anticipatory meaning of resurrection in the theological category of *eschatology*. The biblical roots of eschatology, the key developments regarding eschatology in modern theology, and eschatology's place in Panneberg's overall thought will be discussed. Next, we will examine the critical and constructive role eschatology plays in Pannenberg's theology. Third, we will examine Pannenberg's eschatology as presented in his 1983 Ingersoll Lecture on Immortality and discuss the various assessments made of this lecture.

Eschatology in the Bible

Zachary Hayes offers a useful summary of the issues involved in a discussion of *eschatology*, which is literally a study of or view about the end of history.

Christians are people of hope. But they are not alone in this, for hope is a common element in human experience. What distinguishes Christians is not the mere fact that they hope, but the peculiar way in which they hope and the distinctive reasons for which they hope. In the Scriptures, the object of Christian hope is called the Kingdom of God. The ground for Christian hope is that which God has done in Jesus of Nazareth for the salvation of the world. Here, in seminal form, is the heart of the Christian faith. It is from this center that theology attempts to explicate the vision which Christian hope has for the future of the world.[7]

Christians rest their hope for the future on what God has done through Jesus of Nazareth, but the content of that hope varies from one Christian group to the next. What does the future hold? What significance does that future have for the present? What is the Kingdom of God?

The roots of biblical eschatology are found in the ancient concept of a *covenant,* a binding pledge between God and Israel, expressed simply as "I will take you as my people, and I will be your God" (Exodus 6:7). This divine promise was inextricably linked with the promise of the land of Canaan. But as Richard H. Hiers notes,

Then came a series of oppressors and conquerors. In 721 BC, the Assyrians totally defeated Israel, and in 586 BC, the Babylonians overcame the surviving kingdom of Judah, destroying Jerusalem and the Temple, and carrying most of the Jews into exile. Pre-exilic prophets interpreted these disasters as God's judgment against his people for worshiping other gods and failing to do justice and mercy (e.g., Amos 4-8; Hos. 4-10; Jer. 2-8). Generally these prophets also expected God to punish foreign nations for their false religion, pride, and wickedness (e.g., Isa. 38; Jer. 46; Ezek. 30). Most of them promised that God would restore the fortunes of Israel and Judah afterwards. Oracles of future redemption envisioned not only the restoration of national strength and status but also the establishment of an era of everlasting peace and blessing (e.g., Hos 2:14-23; Isa. 2:2-4; 11; 35; Jer.31:1-37; Ezek. 16:53-63).[8]

These passages predicting an era of everlasting peace and blessing (especially the Immanuel passages in Isaiah) would profoundly shape early Christian proclamation.

A second development in the Old Testament that would exert a significant influence on Christian thought was the rise of apocalyptic thinking. The word *apocalyptic* refers to the revelations granted, usually in symbolic form, to an individual regarding the unalterable course of human history. The message of apocalypse is that God, for reasons unknown to us, has allowed evil nations to oppress the righteous ones of the Lord but that their dominion will soon be overturned in spectacular fashion by God. These signs are being observed at the present time, so the righteous ones who are being persecuted need to persevere in their struggle in the hope that God will soon intervene in human history and bring all people to judgment. That judgment could be carried out by God, or God could delegate authority to another figure (such as the Son of Man). Before that judgment, however, there will be a time of great tribulation. This time of tribulation was commonly compared to the pangs of labor experienced by an expectant mother before she gives birth (see Mark 13:8). This apocalyptic outlook, evident in Daniel 7, also appears in various passages in the gospels and letters and most dramatically in the book of Revelation.

It is also in the apocalyptic tradition that we first see in the Old Testament a belief in the future resurrection of the dead. Daniel 12:2 is often cited as the first instance of this belief in the Old Testament: "Many of those who sleep in the dust of the earth shall awake, some to everlasting life, and some to shame and everlasting contempt." In the New Testament, Paul speaks of Christ's resurrection as "the first fruits of those who have died" (1 Corinthians 15:20). This agricultural metaphor compares the initial harvest of a crop and its relation to an assured, imminent, and abundant harvest with the resurrection of Christ and the hope of future resurrection of "those who belong to Christ" (1 Corinthians 15:23) that will follow the *parousia*, or return of Christ.

All of this helps the modern interpreter form his or her own opinion about the eschatological teachings of Jesus. Modern biblical scholarship has reached a consensus that Jesus' teachings centered on the coming of the kingdom of God (or its equivalent expressions "reign of God" and "kingdom of heaven"). In Mark's gospel, Jesus' opening proclamation is "The time is fulfilled, and the kingdom of God has come near; repent, and believe in the good news" (1:15). What did Jesus preach by this proclamation? Did Christ expect the imminent end of the world as we know it? Was Jesus speaking in spiritual terms or political terms or both? To what extent did Jesus think and act apocalyptically?

These questions have been at the center of New Testament studies for decades, and there is no indication that they will be supplanted anytime soon. To add greater confusion, the gospels seem to give clues leading in different directions. At times, Jesus speaks of the kingdom as a present reality in rather unapocalyptic terms, as in this passage from Luke: "Once Jesus was asked by the Pharisees when the kingdom of God was coming, and he answered, 'The kingdom of God is not coming with things that can be observed; nor will they say, "Look, here it is!" or "There it is!" For, in fact, the kingdom of God is among you'" (17:20-21). On other occasions, Jesus speaks in starkly apocalyptic tones: "Truly I tell you, there are some standing here who will not taste death until they see that the kingdom of God has come with power" (Mark 9:1; see also Mark 13).

Eschatology in Modern Theology

A brief history of the twists and turns of modern biblical scholarship on the question of Jesus' eschatological outlook will lead us directly to Pannenberg's place in that tradition. In Protestant liberalism, the eschatological dimension of Jesus' teachings was either minimized or eliminated. Norman Perrin offers the following assessment of the work of one of the leading voices of that tradition, the nineteenth-century theologian Albrecht Ritschl:

> In all of this the Kingdom of God is conceived by Ritschl in purely ethical terms. Jesus saw in the Kingdom of God the moral task to be carried out by the human race, and . . . it is the organization of humanity through action inspired by love. Christianity itself is completely spiritual and thoroughly ethical. It is completely spiritual in freedom given to the children of God through redemption, which involves the impulse to conduct through the motive of love—and it is thoroughly ethical in that this conduct is directed towards the moral organization of mankind, the establishment of the Kingdom of God.[9]

The challenge to Ritschl came from one of his students who was also his son-in-law, Johannes Weiss. Weiss insisted that his former teacher had not given sufficient attention to the eschatological and apocalyptic elements in Jesus' preaching and had overemphasized the human involvement in the bringing about of the Kingdom of God. Modern biblical scholarship has generally attempted to do justice to both the present and the future dimensions in Jesus' preaching about the Kingdom of God (compare Luke 11:20 and 13:29). For example, Perrin writes in a later work, "In the teaching of Jesus the emphasis is not upon a future for which men must prepare, even with the help of God; the emphasis is upon a present which carries with it the guarantee of the future. The present that has become

God's present guarantees that all futures will be God's future."[10]

One twentieth-century biblical scholar who was a "notable exception to the developing tendency among scholars to recognize the Kingdom as both present and future in the teaching of Jesus"[11] was Rudolf Bultmann, whose work we discussed briefly in chapter 4 on Bonhoeffer. For Bultmann, Jesus' preaching centered on the future coming of the Kingdom. This may seem a liability, since it leaves open the possibility that Jesus mistakenly expected the imminent end of the world. Bultmann, however, sees this future aspect of Jesus' preaching as the perfect complement to modern existentialist thought. Bultmann writes, "Rather, the Kingdom of God is a power *which, although it is entirely future, wholly determines the present*. It determines the present because it now compels man to decision; he is determined thereby either in this direction or in that, as chosen or as rejected, in his present existence."[12]

Bultmann's strategy was to uncover the existential message embedded in the mythological language of the New Testament writings. Given the nature of the gospels as faith documents, he did not feel the historical accuracy of individual sayings or incidents could be definitively determined. More importantly, Bultmann believed that Christian faith does not rest on the Jesus of history but rather on the Christ of faith. It is the risen Christ who confronts us in Christian preaching, and it is the risen Christ who challenges us with the existential decision to place our trust in a power beyond ourselves in order to live authentic human lives.

Hermeneutical Theology

The rediscovery of the apocalyptic character of Jesus' preaching presented a problem for modern theologians: How can those of us in the modern age who no longer hold an apocalyptic outlook understand a message that is ancient and apocalyptic in character without distorting the message itself? This is the question that gives rise to *hermeneutics*, the technical term for the process of interpretation.

"[The] central problem of hermeneutics," writes Pannenberg, "[concerns] the distance between primitive Christianity and our age."[13] Pannenberg sees in the apocalyptic expectation of the early Christians not an obstacle for modern Christians to overcome as much as a valuable resource for them to contemplate. Apocalyptic thinkers see history as the locus of God's revelation and live their lives in the present world in light of the future promised by God. Both of these apocalyptic elements feature prominently in Pannenberg's theology.

The Place of Eschatology in Pannenberg's Theology

Pannenberg places eschatology at the center of his theology. More specifically, he highlights the importance of apocalyptic thinking for Christian faith. In an early programmatic essay, Pannenberg insists that "it is only within this tradition of prophetic and apocalyptic expectation that it is possible to understand the resurrection of Jesus and his pre-Easter life as a reflection of the eschatological self-vindication of Jahweh."[14] In another early influential essay, "Theology and the Kingdom of God," Pannenberg situates his work in the modern history of biblical scholarship. He writes,

> From Kant to Ritschl and the religious socialists, the Kingdom of God and its propagation were goals to be achieved though man's labor. Today such thinking is dismissed as being simplistic or even dangerously naive. But theologians of the past correctly asserted that where men comply with the will of God, there is the Kingdom

of God. Taking this a step farther, they asserted that to extend the sphere of obedience to God's will means the extension and establishment of his Kingdom.

This assumption was upset by Johannes Weiss toward the end of the nineteenth century. He discovered that, according to the New Testament and Jesus' message, the Kingdom of God will be established not by men but by God alone. The coming of the Kingdom will involve cosmic revolutions and change far beyond anything conceivable as a consequence of man's progressive labor. God will establish his Kingdom unilaterally. Therefore Jesus, and John the Baptizer before him, only announced the Kingdom of God, exposing every present condition under the light of the imminent future. This future is expected to come in a marvelous way from God himself; it is not simply the development of human history or achievement of God-fearing men.[15]

Pannenberg then concludes, "This resounding motif of Jesus' message—the imminent Kingdom of God—must be recovered as a key to the whole of Christian theology."[16] We will focus on three features of Pannenberg's theology that take seriously "this resounding motif of Jesus' message."

First, Pannenberg gives theological priority to the future. As he states in his *Systematic Theology*,

The truth of the revelation of God in Jesus Christ is dependent, then, on the actual in-breaking of the future of God's kingdom, and we maintain and declare it today on the premise of that coming. The coming of the kingdom is the basis of the message of Jesus, and without the arrival of this future it loses its basis. . . . As the work and history of Jesus were essentially an anticipation of this reign, and as they depend on the future of the ultimate coming for their meaning and truth, so do the liturgical life of the church, the presence of Jesus Christ at celebrations of his Supper, and the saving efficacy of baptism, along with the Christian sense of election and faith's assurance of justification. As regards its content and truth all Christian doctrine depends on the future of God's own coming to consummate his rule over his creation.[17]

Pannenberg declares that Christianity is based on a divine promise. If the promise is not kept, then the framework of Christian belief and practice will crumble. The future is, of course, not unrelated to the present. In fact, much like a mariner charts a course based on the final destination, the Christian sees every day against the backdrop of God's kingdom that is yet to come. Christians' eschatological hope is that "what turns out to be true in the future will then be evident as having been true all along," according to Pannenberg.[18]

Second, the Christian life is characterized by anticipation. Simply stated, "In the fate of Jesus, the end of history is experienced in advance as an anticipation."[19] The concept of anticipation is so important to Pannenberg's theology that Philip Clayton labels it "the central systematic principle of his theology." Clayton writes,

> It was thinking through the logic of Jesus' resurrection, along with the resultant authority of his message and divinity of his person, that led Pannenberg to the central systematic principle of his theology, the concept of anticipation. As the apocalyptic horizon criterion suggests, *the anticipatory structure that characterizes most of what Pannenberg has written is generalized directly from the conclusions of his Christology.*[20]

The resurrection is a taste, a glimpse, or a down payment. Christians live by the faith that the end of history has been previewed in Christ.

The third feature of Pannenberg's theology that follows from his eschatological focus is the provisional view of human endeavors. As Richard John Neuhaus explains,

Provisionality in Pannenberg's thought is not a condition that excuses a lack of commitment. This is as true of the intellectual life as it is of commitment to social change. That is, we must have the maturity to recognize the tentative character of existence on the one hand and the urgency of embracing it as the only existence we have on the other. For many, not only for Christians, there is an unbreakable connection between commitment and certitude; we can only be thoroughly committed to what we are absolutely sure about. Christians frequently appeal to some authority, revelation perhaps, to establish the certitude of the premises on which they act. To Pannenberg's radically provisional view of existence it is objected that if we cannot know for sure, we cannot act with religious seriousness. Pannenberg counters that religious faith is connected not so much to certitude as it is to venturing risk on the basis of reasonable probabilities.[21]

Pannenberg explains, "A commitment to the provisional is essential to Christian faith in the Kingdom of God. To withhold such a commitment because the absolute remains out of reach of human endeavors would mean betraying the Kingdom. And yet it is the special contribution of the eschatological understanding of the Kingdom that it does not allow any particular social program to be mistaken for the Kingdom."[22] The eschatological orientation, therefore, translates into neither social indifference nor theocratic politics.

"Constructive and Critical Functions of Christian Eschatology"

We can now delve into Pannenberg's Ingersoll Lecture on Immortality, delivered at the Harvard Divinity School on October 13, 1983. The lecture consists of a brief introduction and four sections. In the space of twenty pages, the lecture summarizes nicely the themes we have been discussing so far in Pannenberg's theology.

In the first part of the lecture, Pannenberg comments on the traditional grouping of biblical images about the end of time into individual and social eschatology. He notes, "Individual eschatology focuses on a future life of the individual in terms of bodily resurrection, immortality of the soul, and communion with God and with Christ. In the center of social eschatology there is the hope for the kingdom of God that will bring about true justice and peace among all creatures."[23] Karl Rahner, for example, connects his views on human nature as created by God and the fulfillment of that nature in God's kingdom. What is indistinctly known will be made clear in the final consummation. Protestant theologians have shied away from this approach and largely argued in terms of a scheme of promise fulfillment based on divine promises contained in Scripture. Pannenberg sees both approaches as preserving an important ingredient in any Christian eschatology. The future will bring about human fulfillment so that the fulfillment will bear a resemblance to the present state of humans, and, of course, that fulfillment will take place at the time and in the manner determined by God.

In the second part of the lecture, Pannenberg addresses the common criticism that eschatology introduces an otherworldly element to Christian faith, which Karl Marx rightly criticized. This otherworldly dimension encourages those individuals who are suffering political, social, or economic injustice to quietly endure their hardship in the hope that they will be rewarded in heaven. Pannenberg counters,

In declaring the consummation of human existence to be a matter of hope beyond death, religious eschatology denounces the illusions of secular belief in the attainability of a perfect and unambiguous happiness in this world. In proclaiming the eschatological kingdom of God to be the place of the achievement of true peace and justice among human beings, Christian eschatology denounces at the same time the pretensions of the politicians who claim that by taking the measures they advocate, ultimate justice and perfect peace could be achieved in our secular societies.[24]

In other words, this otherworldliness does not reduce Christian faith to escapism or social indifference but rather serves as the standard by which to judge the present state of the world. This is the vital, *critical* function of Christian eschatology. Rather than deny the world, "it clears the stage for a realistic involvement in its struggles, without admitting illusions of obtaining ultimate solutions to its problems and without the psychological need for considering the opponent as a foe of the ultimate truth itself."[25]

With the struggle for social justice comes the inevitable frustration, despair, or sense of being overwhelmed. Here, Christian eschatology plays a *constructive* function. Pannenberg writes, "Eschatological hope empowers the individual to carry the burden of its finite existence with all its irremovable limitations and disgraceful frustrations. It encourages the human person to face the evils of this world as they are, without illusion. Hope . . . illumines the present existence in spite of its shortcomings."[26]

The eschatological backdrop of Christian faith provides the standard by which the conditions of the world are measured (the critical function) and is the source of hope for those struggling to bring about that better world (the constructive function). It shatters the illusion that any government or human cause represents the unambiguous fulfillment of divine promises (the critical function) yet calls on all humans to organize their efforts to address the urgent needs of their fellow human beings (the constructive function).

How, then, should we view the end of time? What is the content of Christian hope? Pannenberg addresses these questions in the third part of his Ingersoll lecture when he turns his attention to the "problem of how a life beyond death can be conceived."[27]

The Christian tradition has preserved two ways of conceiving the future life of an individual beyond death: a future resurrection of the body and an immortal soul. Both provide a means for speaking about a real continuity between a person's identity in this life and the next. The former belief—a hope in a future resurrected body—is found in Paul's letters (for instance, 1 Corinthians 15; 1 Thessalonians 4). The latter belief of the immortal soul figured prominently in Greek philosophy and was incorporated into Christian thought, according to Pannenberg, to handle the vexing problem of how to maintain a belief in personal survival long after the corpse had decomposed. The immortal soul provided the mechanism for preserving personal identity over the long expanse of time between a person's death and the general resurrection at the end of time.

Pannenberg sees human identity as derived from both body and soul, so the resurrected state must include both. Between now and the end of time, we remain present to the Lord. "What happens in the moment of death, then, is that we are no longer present to ourselves, nor to other creatures, although we remain present to God. It is this inextinguishable presence to God's eternity that provides the condition of the possibility that the same life of ours can come alive again."[28]

What exactly would such an event entail? Pannenberg now advances his own position regarding this future event.

Assessments of Pannenberg's Ingersoll Lecture on Immortality

Pannenberg develops his position in response to the criticisms of theologian John Hick.[29] Since Pannenberg has ruled out the mind's disembodied survival of death, argues Hick, then the resuscitation of a corpse in this world would be no less impossible. Pannenberg replies that if our life remains with God, then the restoration of some type of self-awareness to those who have died would be similar to the original act of creation by God.[30]

Second, Hick wonders whether Pannenberg's view of eternal life would be nothing more than an eternal reminder of all the evils and tragedies that have befallen a person in his or her earthly life. Pannenberg believes Hick "underestimates the implications of the *transformation* that occurs to the finite life in light of eternity."[31] This involves both judgment and glorification. Writes Pannenberg, "Eternal judgment does not mean a violent reaction of a punishing God against his creatures. It rather means that the sinner is left to the consequences of his or her own behavior."[32] Eternal bliss arises when a person sees his or her own life as a participation in the life of God. "The presence of God means glorification as well as judgment, and whether it will be one or the other depends on the relation of the creature to God and to his kingdom."[33]

Hick's third objection is prompted by his interest in world religions. He sees in Pannenberg's theology a link between salvation and the gospel message. Hick argues, "Such a doctrine can only apply to those who have lived to responsible maturity during the centuries since Jesus lived and in the lands in which his gospel has been known. It cannot apply . . . to those who have lived before Jesus or outside the influence of historic Christianity; and yet these of course constitute the large majority of the human race."[34] Pannenberg believes such a problem disappears if "Jesus and his message are considered to stand as a *criterion* of God's eternal judgment, but not as the indispensable *means*, the explicit acceptance of which would be a precondition of participation in the kingdom of God."[35]

The Future of Hermeneutical Theology

In the article "Beyond Criticism," the Scripture scholars and theologians Ellen F. Davis and Richard B. Hays make this observation:

> The difficulty of interpreting the Bible is felt not only in secular culture but also in the church at the beginning of the 21st century. Is the Bible authoritative for the faith and practice of the church. Is so, in what way? What practices of reading offer the most appropriate approach to understanding the Bible? How does historical criticism illumine or obscure scripture's message? How are premodern Christian readings to be brought into engagement with historical methodologies, as well as feminist, liberationist and postmodernist readings? The church's lack of clarity about these issues has hindered its witness and mission, so that it fails to speak with wisdom, imagination and courage to the challenges of our time.[36]

Davis and Hays's list of questions not only serves as an agenda for future hermeneutical theology but also incorporates many of the issues we have discussed throughout the book. These questions address just some of the challenges confronting Christian theologians at the beginning of the twenty-first century.

The End of Time

The fourth and final part of Pannenberg's lecture deals with the notion of an end of history. Pannenberg insists that "the end of time does not border on some other time, but the notion of an end of time expresses the finite character of time as such."[37] Pannenberg instead suggests that "God himself is the end of time, and as the end of time he is the final future of his creation. This does not entail the annihilation of time, but the lifting up of temporal histories into the form of an eternal presence."[38] Pannenberg does not believe it is necessary to view the end as an obliteration of all distinctions; rather, he proposes that we view the end as a communion with God in eschatological glory. In the meantime, "We travel through the history of our lives in the light of some continuing presence that travels with us."[39]

Discussion Questions

1. How do you believe the world will end? Will certain events signal that the end is near? Do you interpret biblical language about Jesus returning on the clouds of heaven literally or figuratively?

2. In what concrete ways do beliefs about the end of time influence how we live in the present?

3. How does Christian eschatology help free the Christian to involve himself or herself in the affairs of this world? In your opinion, what are the critical and constructive uses of Christian eschatology?

4. On what is Christian hope for the future based? Is it a promise in Scripture, the general direction of human history, or some element of human nature?

5. Do you believe that the human personality will survive death in some form? If so, in what form? If not, why not?

Notes

1. Stanley J. Grenz and Roger E. Olson, *Twentieth-Century Theology* (Downers Grove, Ill.: InterVarsity Press, 1992), p. 189.

2. Wolfhart Pannenberg, "Introduction," in Wolfart Pannenberg, ed., *Revelation as History* (London: Collier-Macmillan, 1968), p. 19.

3. James C. Livingston and Francis Schüssler Fiorenza, *Modern Christian Thought*, 2nd ed., vol. 2 (Minneapolis: Fortress Press, 2006), p. 344.

4. Livingston and Fiorenza, *Modern Christian Thought*, p. 345.

5. Wolfhart Pannenberg, "God's Presence in History," *Christian Century* 98, no. 8 (March 11, 1981): 261.

6. Ed. L. Miller and Stanley J. Grenz, *Fortress Introduction to Contemporary Theologies* (Minneapolis: Fortress Press, 1998), p. 127.

7. Zachary Hayes, *Visions of the Future* (Collegeville, Minn.: Liturgical Press, 1990), p. 15.

8. Richard H. Hiers, "Eschatology," in Paul J. Achtemeier, ed., *Harper's Bible Dictionary* (San Francisco: Harper & Row, 1985), pp. 275–276.

9. Norman Perrin, *The Kingdom of God in the Teachings of Jesus* (Philadelphia: Westminster Press, 1963), p. 16.

10. Norman Perrin, *Rediscovering the Teaching of Jesus* (New York: Harper & Row, 1976), p. 205.

11. Perrin, *The Kingdom of God*, p. 112.

12. Rudolf Bultmann, *Jesus and the Word* (New York: Charles Scribner's, 1958), p. 51. Italics in original.

13. Wolhart Pannenberg, "Hermeneutics and Universal History," in Robert Funk, ed., *History and Hermeneutic* (New York: Harper & Row, 1967), p. 122.

14. Wolfhart Pannenberg, "Dogmatic Theses on the Doctrine of Revelation," in Wolfhart Pannenberg, ed., *Revelation as History* (London: Collier-Macmillan, 1968), p. 127.

15. Wolfhart Pannenberg, "Theology and the Kingdom of God," in Richard John Neuhaus, ed., *Theology and the Kingdom of God* (Philadelphia: Westminster Press, 1969), pp. 51–52.

16. Pannenberg, "Theology and the Kingdom of God," p. 53.

17. Wolfhart Pannenberg, *Systematic Theology*, vol. 3 (Grand Rapids, Mich.: William B. Eerdmans, 1998), p. 531.

18. Pannenberg, "Theology and the Kingdom of God," p. 63. Critics have rightly pointed out the tension in Pannenberg's theology on this point. At times, he speaks of history as open ended, with God being affected by the course of history. At other times, he speaks of God as unaffected by history. See Philip Clayton, "Anticipation and Theological Method," in Carl E. Braaten and Philip Clayton, eds., *The Theology of Wolfhart Pannenberg* (Minneapolis: Fortress Press, 1988), pp. 139–140.

19. Pannenberg, "Dogmatic Theses," p. 134.

20. Clayton, "Anticipation and Theological Method," p. 131. Emphasis in original.

21. Richard John Neuhaus, "Wolfhart Pannenberg: Profile of a Theologian," in Richard John Neuhaus, ed., *Theology and the Kingdom of God* (Philadelphia: Westminster, 1969), pp. 19–20.

22. Wolfhart Pannenberg, "The Kingdom of God and the Foundation of Ethics," in Richard John Neuhaus, ed., *Theology and the Kingdom of God* (Philadelphia: Westminster, 1969), pp. 114–115.

23. Wolfhart Pannenberg, "Constructive and Critical Functions of Christian Eschatology," *Harvard Theological Review* 77, no. 2 (1984): 120.

24. Pannenberg, "Constructive and Critical Functions," p. 124.

25. Ibid., p. 124.

26. Ibid.

27. Ibid., p. 128.

28. Ibid., p. 131.

29. Hick's criticisms can be found in his work *Death and Eternal Life* (San Francisco: Harper & Row, 1976), pp. 221–226. See also Hick's response to Pannenberg's lecture in his "A Note on Pannenberg's Eschatology," *Harvard Theological Review* 77 (1984): 421–423.

30. Pannenberg, "Constructive and Critical Functions," p. 133.

31. Ibid., p. 134. Italics in original.

32. Ibid., p. 134.

33. Ibid., p. 135.

34. Hick, *Death and Eternal Life*, p. 225.

35. Pannenberg, "Constructive and Critical Functions," p. 136. Italics in original.

36. Ellen F. Davis and Richard B. Hays, "Beyond Criticism," *Christian Century* 121, no. 8 (April 20, 2004): 23.

37. Pannenberg, "Constructive and Critical Functions," p. 137.

38. Ibid., p. 138.

39. Ibid.

⊚ Suggested Readings

For a brief introduction to the theme of eschatology, see "Eschatology: Conceptions of," by Josef Finkenzeller, and "Eschatology: Contemporary Issues," by Roger Haight, both in Wolfgang Beinert and Francis Schüssler Fiorenza, eds., *Handbook of Catholic Theology* (New York: Crossroad, 1995). See also Carl E. Braaten, "The Kingdom of God and the Life Everlasting," in Peter C. Hodgson and Robert H. King, eds., *Christian Theology* (Philadelphia: Fortress Press, 1982), and "David Fergusson, "Eschatology," in Colin E. Gunton, ed., *The Cambridge Companion to Christian Doctrine* (Cambridge: Cambridge University Press, 1997). For a book-length treatment, see Zachary Hayes, *Visions of a Future* (Collegeville, Minn.: Liturgical Press, 1989).

For an introduction to Pannenberg's theology, see Carl E. Braaten, "Wolfhart Pannenberg," in Martin Marty and Dean G. Peerman, eds., *A Handbook of Christian Theologians*, enlarged ed. (Nashville, Tenn.: Abingdon Press, 1984), and Richard John Neuhaus, "Wolfhart Pannenberg: Profile of a Theologian," in *Theology and the Kingdom of God* (Philadelphia: Westminster, 1969). Another helpful resource is the master's thesis of Brian John Walsh, *Futurity and Creation* (Toronto: Institute for Christian Studies, 1979).

Students in upper-level courses who are looking for treatments of Pannenberg's eschatology should read Philip Clayton, "Anticipation and Theological Method," and Ted Peters, "Pannenberg's Eschatological Ethics," both in Carl E. Braaten and Philip Clayton, eds., *The Theology of Wolfhart Pannenberg* (Minneapolis: Augsburg, 1988). Also helpful in that volume is Stanley Grenz, "The Appraisal of Pannenberg: A Survey of the Literature." See also chapter 6 of Stanley Grenz, *Reason for Hope* (New York: Oxford University Press, 1990). Another helpful but difficult resource is E. Frank Tupper, *The Theology of Wolfhart Pannenberg* (Philadelphia: Westminster Press, 1973), chapters 8 and 9.

Thinking about Theology

We have examined works by ten of the most influential thinkers in the field of contemporary theology. Obviously, other theologians and other movements within contemporary theology could have been selected. (See the appendix for a listing of other contemporary theologians.) However, these ten theologians give us a glimpse of the diversity that presently exists within Christian theology.

What assistance can these thinkers offer to readers in their future theological studies? The answer, I suggest, can be found by thinking of the work of the theologians in terms of the practice of medicine and by asking three vital questions: What is the diagnosis? What is the prescription? What are the alternative treatments?[1]

Rosemary Radford Ruether and other feminist thinkers focus their research on the problem of sexism. Ruether finds this malady has infected both Scripture and many of the classic works in Western theology, and she prescribes an egalitarian understanding of human persons, of the wider society, and of God. Some fellow Christian theologians who agree with her diagnosis believe that her proposals give too much weight to experience and not enough weight to the authority of Scripture and therefore seek remedies that would preserve a greater role for the Bible.

Gustavo Gutiérrez and other liberation theologians believe that the Christian community has lost its ability to see clearly its responsibility to the wider society. Given the church's problem with its vision, Gutiérrez proposes that Christians view the Scriptures through the lens of liberation; doing so will bring the plight of the poor into sharper focus. Critics fear that such a solution blurs the necessary distinction between religion and politics.

Reinhold Niebuhr and his fellow Christian realists focus on the frozen grip of those who cling to power in society. To loosen a clenched fist, argue the realists, we must first apply pressure. Like a physical therapy that involves painful stretching of the muscle, social change often requires the skillful use of power. Critics charge that such an approach often endorses a course of treatment that is incompatible with Christian ethics.

Inspired by the cryptic sayings of Dietrich Bonhoeffer, secular theologians fear that the modern world is growing deaf to the voice of God. Furthermore, the secular world seems to refuse the treatment offered in the Christian gospel. If this is the case, how should we proceed? Shouting, the secular theologians contend, is not the answer. Instead, we need to find a language that is responsive to the actual questions being asked by our contemporaries. Critics sense that this amounts to contributing to "the death of God."

Sallie McFague and the liberal theologians see a diseased ecological situation. Because this is a rapidly progressing illness, they call for urgent action. The cause is the outdated understanding we have of the relationship between God and the world. The theologian must construct models of God that can address the underlying causes of our present ecological plight. As these proposals grow increasingly imaginative, however, critics fear that we can easily drift away from traditional, time-honored beliefs and practices and adopt those that have in the past proven harmful to the ecclesiastical body.

Karl Rahner and the other neo-Thomists attempt to express traditional beliefs in a manner that accords with modern conceptions of the mind. Just as breakthroughs in medical research allow us to approach problems from new angles, developments in theology and philosophy help us to approach traditional beliefs from a new standpoint, one that may be more intelligible to contemporary Christians. Rahner's critics, however, insist that these new developments have also called into question some of the foundational assumptions underlying his proposals.

Jürgen Moltmann and the political theologians concentrate our attention on the problem of suffering. Just as the medical community simultaneously treats the individual and engages in discussion regarding public health, the theological community needs to address the issue of suffering on both individual and social levels. Moltmann recommends that Christians understand the crucifixion as a moment in the very life of God. Critics contend that such a move does not offer us much hope but simply infects God with the same disease.

Stanley Hauerwas and the postliberal theologians remind us that medicine, theology, and other disciplines comprise sets of skills that we acquire by being initiated into the guild, learning the language of the craft, and embodying the truths of the tradition in our way of life. For Christians, this nonviolent way of life is grounded in the life, death, and resurrection of Christ. Critics believe that an insular way of life is unhealthy and that the Christian community needs to be willing to alter its way of life when the evidence warrants it.

Before a patient undergoes a potentially life-altering procedure, the doctor encourages him or her to get a second opinion. What is the best course of action if the second opinion offers a different diagnosis than the first? What if a third and fourth opinion are sought, and they offer conflicting diagnoses and recommendations? What course of action should the individual choose? Pluralism can be paralyzing. John Cobb Jr. grapples with the issue of religious pluralism through the use of the Logos. Determining the best method of dealing with the competing truth claims of the world's religions remains one of the most daunting tasks that contemporary theologians face.[2]

Wolfhart Pannenberg and the hermeneutical theologians call our attention to the fact that any diagnosis or prescription requires that we both understand the past and look toward the future. Christian theologians must properly interpret the past, especially the teachings of Jesus regarding the Kingdom of God, yet also anticipate the state of affairs that will exist at the end of time. Critics may take issue with either one or both ends of the time line. They could either disagree with Pannenberg's account of Jesus' teachings or offer an alternative vision of the final consummation of history.

Future Theological Study

As readers critically evaluate theological ideas and proposals, they can ask themselves the three questions we applied to each theologian: What is the diagnosis? What is the prescription? What are the alternative treatments? In terms of the diagnosis, what is the problem we confront? What are its causes? In terms of the prescription, what are the options for solving the problem? What factors should be given the greatest consideration? Finally, what are the shortcomings of the proposals? What are the chief strengths of the opponent's position? In this way, we can help ourselves and others wrestle with the questions in contemporary theology.

⊚ Notes

1. I am borrowing from a similar approach in Leslie Stevenson, *Seven Theories of Human Nature*, 2nd ed. (New York: Oxford University Press, 1987).

2. For a brief reflection on this point, see the work of another influential theologian of the twentieth century, H. Richard Niebuhr, in *Christ and Culture* (New York: Harper & Row, 1951), pp. 234–241.

Appendix of Additional Theologians

Below are listed some other theologians, contemporary and recent, whose work has been especially influential in contemporary Christian thought, along with samples of their works. There is a great deal of "cross-pollination" among various theological schools of thought. A theologian can be representative of any combination of the ten theological movements discussed in the text, for example, liberation and feminist and black theologies. Lines between Catholic and Protestant theology have also often blurred to the point where a liberal Catholic may have more in common with a liberal Protestant than with a conservative Catholic. The categories below, then, are meant to associate the theologians with those groups that, it is hoped, they themselves might accept as appropriately descriptive of their work and orientation.

Ecumenical Theologies

Robert W. Jenson (1930–). Lutheran. Though deeply influenced by Karl Barth and Continental thought, Jenson is an example of a theologian working in terms of an explicitly ecumenical theology.

- *Systematic Theology.* 2 vols. New York: Oxford University Press, 1997, 1999.
- *Story and Promise: A Brief Theology of the Gospel about Jesus,* Philadelphia: Fortress Press, 1973.
- *Unbaptized God: The Basic Flaw in Ecumenical Theology.* Philadelphia: Fortress Press, 1992.

George A. Lindbeck (1923–). Lutheran. While at Yale Divinity School, Lindbeck provided important initial work for postliberalism as well as a new framework for ecumenical relations.

- *The Nature of Doctrine: Religion and Theology in a Postliberal Age.* Philadelphia: Westminster Press, 1984.
- *The Church in a Postliberal Age.* Ed. James J. Buckley. Grand Rapids, Mich.: Eerdmans, 2003.

Evangelical Protestant Theologies

Karl Barth (1886–1968). Reformed Church/Calvinist. Barth's theology continues to influence contemporary theology through his emphasis on the biblical narrative as the sole framework for Christian theology.

- *Dogmatics in Outline.* Trans. G.T. Thompson. New York: Harper and Row, 1959.
- *Evangelical Theology: An Introduction.* Trans. Grover Foley. New York: Holt, Rinehart, and Winston, 1963.

Carl F. H. Henry (1913–2003). Baptist. The dean of American evangelical Protestant theology, his work remains its authoritative expression.

- *God, Revelation, and Authority.* 6 vols. Waco, Tex.: Word Books, 1976–83.

Liberal and Reformist Protestant Theologies

Hans W. Frei (1922–1988). Episcopalian. At the center of the emergence of postliberal theology at Yale.

- *The Eclipse of Biblical Narrative: A Study in Eighteenth and Nineteenth Century Hermeneutics.* New Haven, Conn.: Yale University Press, 1974.

Douglas John Hall (1928–) United Church of Canada. A student of both Niebuhr and Tillich, Hall has forged an explicitly North American theology in light of the waning influence of denominational Christianity in an increasingly secularized culture.

- Trilogy: Christian Theology in a North American Context: *Thinking the Faith, Professing the Faith, Confessing the Faith.* Minneapolis: Fortress Press, 1989, 1993, 1996.
- *The Cross in Our Context: Jesus and the Suffering World.* Minneapolis: Fortress Press, 2003.

Peter C. Hodgson (1934–). Presbyterian. Now retired from Vanderbilt University, Hodgson is one of the leading liberal Protestant voices in American theology.

- *Winds of the Spirit: A Constructive Christian Theology.* Louisville, Ky.: Westminster John Knox, 1994.
- *God in History: Shapes of Freedom.* Nashville, Tenn.: Abingdon Press, 1989.

Gordon D. Kaufman (1925–). Mennonite. This Harvard theologian has pioneered constructive theology in a Kantian, postfoundational vein, especially on the meaning of God.

- *God—Mystery—Diversity: Christian Theology in a Pluralistic World.* Minneapolis: Fortress Press, 1996.
- *In Face of Mystery: A Constructive Theology.* Cambridge, Mass.: Harvard University Press, 1993.

Kosuke Koyama (1929–). Presbyterian. A Japanese-born theologian, Koyama taught in Asia, East Asia, and the United States, and is professor emeritus at Union Theological

Seminary in New York City. He has produced a distinctively Asian theology.

- *Water Buffalo Theology*. Maryknoll, N.Y.: Orbis Books, 1999 [1974].

John Macquarrie (1919–2007). Episcopal/Anglican Communion. Macquarrie's important work combined themes in existentialist philosophy with Christian theology.

- *The Principles of Christian Theology*. New York: Charles Scribner's Sons, 1966.

Paul Ricoeur (1913–2005*)*. Protestant. Ricoeur's work has deeply affected Christian theological understandings of hermeneutics and philosophical theology.

- *The Symbolism of Evil*. Trans. Emerson Buchanan. New York: Harper & Row, 1967.
- *Time and Narrative*. 3 vols. Trans. Kathleen McLaughlin and David Pellauer. Chicago: University of Chicago Press, 1984–88.

Dorothee Soelle (1929–2003). Evangelical Church of Germany. Arriving in New York City in 1975, Soelle taught at Union Theological Seminary for thirteen years. Her work strongly shaped political theology, feminist theology, and ecological theology.

- *Theology for Skeptics: Reflections on God*. Trans. Joyce L. Irwin. Minneapolis: Fortress Press, 1995.
- *The Silent Cry: Mysticism and Resistance*. Trans. Barbara Rumscheidt and Martin Rumscheidt. Minneapolis: Fortress Press, 2001.

Conservative Roman Catholic Theologies

Joseph Ratzinger (1927–). Roman Catholic. Even before becoming Pope Benedict XVI, Ratzinger was a respected conservative Roman Catholic theologian.

- *Introduction to Christianity*. Trans. J. R. Foster. San Francisco: Ignatius Press, 2004 [1970].

Hans Urs von Balthasar (1905–1988). One of the leading Catholic interpreters of Karl Barth's theology, von Balthasar championed a conservative theology that drew extensively on the thought of early church thinkers.

- *The Moment of Christian Witness*. Trans. Richard Beckley. San Francisco: Ignatius Press, 1994 [1969].

Liberal Roman Catholic Theologies

Roger Haight, S.J. (1936–). Roman Catholic. A student of Edward Schillebeeckx, Haight has applied a more inductive method to theology, Christology, and ecclesiology.

- *Dynamics of Theology*. Maryknoll, N.Y.: Orbis Books, 2001 [1990].
- *Jesus: Symbol of God*. Maryknoll, N.Y.: Orbis Books, 1999.

Hans Küng (1928–). Roman Catholic. A theologian at the University of Tübingen, Küng and his work have proven at once prophetic, provocative, and popular; and he remains one of the most influential thinkers in liberal Catholic circles.

- *On Being a Christian*. Trans. Edward Quinn. Garden City, N.Y.: Doubleday, 1976.

Elizabeth A. Johnson (1941–). Roman Catholic. Especially for her creative and systematic integration of feminist and ecological themes with classical *loci*, Johnson's work is both deeply respected and widely read.

- *She Who Is: The Mystery of God in Feminist Theological Discourse.* New York: Crossroad, 2002.
- *Quest for the Living God: Mapping Frontiers in the Theology of God.* New York: Continuum, 2007.

Bernard J.F. Lonergan, S.J. (1904–1984). Roman Catholic. This Canadian Jesuit was one of the most important Catholic interpreters of Thomas Aquinas before turning his attention to bringing historical consciousness and contemporary method to Catholic theology.

- *Insight: A Study of Human Understanding.* 3rd ed. New York: Philosophical Library, 1970 [1957].
- *Method in Theology.* New York: Herder & Herder, 1972.

Thomas Merton (1915–1968). Among the most noted of Catholic authors in the postwar period, Trappist monk Merton's theological writing drew on traditional contemplative theology yet addressed contemporary social concerns, such as the Vietnam War.

- *Seeds of Contemplation.* Westwood, Conn.: Greenwood, 1979.
- *Bread in the Wilderness.* New York: New Directions, 1997.

David Tracy (1939–). Roman Catholic. Perhaps the leading American Roman Catholic theologian, Tracy has taught for a generation at the University of Chicago Divinity School.

- *The Analogical Imagination: Christian Theology and the Culture of Pluralism*. New York: Crossroad, 1981.
- *Talking about God: Doing Theology in the Context of Modern Pluralism*. With John B. Cobb Jr. New York: Seabury Press, 1983.
- *Plurality and Ambiguity: Hermeneutics, Religion, and Hope*. Chicago: University of Chicago Press, 1994.

Latin American Liberation Theologies

Leonardo Boff (1938–). Roman Catholic. A bold and ambitious thinker, Argentinian Boff has tackled major theological topics in a liberation mode, though not without stirring some official opposition.

- *Trinity and Society*. Trans. Paul Burns. Maryknoll, N.Y.: Orbis Books, 1988.
- *Jesus Christ, Liberator: A Critical Christology for Our Time*. Trans. Patrick Hughes. Maryknoll, N.Y.: Orbis Books, 1978.

Ivone Gebara (1944–). Roman Catholic. This Brazilian sister has brought not only gender but also ecology to the fore as key foci of ecofeminist liberation theology.

- *Longing for Running Water: Ecofeminism and Liberation*. Trans. David Molineaux. Minneapolis: Fortress Press, 1999.
- *Out of the Depths: Women's Experience of Evil and Salvation*. Trans. Ann Patrick Ware. Minneapolis: Fortress Press, 2002.

José Míguez Bonino (1924–). Methodist. This Argentinian thinker authored two classic statements on Protestant Latin American liberation theology.

- *Toward a Christian Political Ethics.* Philadelphia: Fortress Press, 1983.
- *Doing Theology in a Revolutionary Situation.* Philadelphia: Fortress Press, 1975.

Juan Luis Segundo, S.J. (1925–1996). Roman Catholic. An Urugayan founder of liberation theology, Segundo particularly explored the intersection of theology, politics, and economics.

- *The Liberation of Theology.* Trans. John Drury. Maryknoll, N.Y.: Orbis Books, 1976.
- *The Liberation of Dogma: Faith, Revelation, and Dogmatic Teaching Authority.* Trans. Phillip Berryman. Maryknoll, N.Y.: Orbis Books, 1992.

Jon Sobrino (1938–) The Basque Jesuit was a founder of the University of Central America, in San Salvador. His chief works, which have been challenged by the Vatican, concern Christology and were forged during the civil unrest in El Salvador.

- *Christ the Liberator: A View from the Victims.* Trans. Paul Burns. Maryknoll, N.Y.: Orbis Books, 2001.
- *Witnesses to the Kingdom: The Martyrs of El Salvador and the Crucified Peoples.* Maryknoll, N.Y.: Orbis Books, 2003.

Elsa Tamez (1950–). Methodist. This Costa Rican theologian has raised a distinctly Protestant feminist voice for liberation theology in Latin America.

- *The Bible of the Oppressed.* Trans. Matthew J. O'Connell. Maryknoll, N.Y.: Orbis Books, 1982.
- *Amnesty of Grace: Justification by Grace from a Latin American Perspective.* Trans. Sharon H. Ringe. Nashville, Tenn.: Abingdon Press, 1993.

Feminist Theologies

Carter Heyward (1945–). Episcopalian. Among the first women ordained to the Episcopal priesthood in 1974, Heyward served for a generation at Episcopal Divinity School, Cambridge, and has explored systematic theology and issues of sexuality and power in feminist theology.

- *Our Passion for Justice: Images of Power, Sexuality, and Liberation.* New York: Pilgrim Press, 1984.
- *Touching Our Strength: The Erotic as Power and Love of God.* San Francisco: Harper & Row, 1989.
- *Saving Jesus: From Those Who Are Right.* Minneapolis: Fortress Press, 1999.

Letty M. Russell (1929–2007). Presbyterian. Yale theologian and feminist pioneer, Russell created a distinctly ecumenical, church-friendly feminism centered solidly in biblical authority and historic Christian traditions.

- *Household of Freedom: Authority in Feminist Theology.* Philadelphia: Westminster Press, 1987.
- *Church in the Round: Feminist Interpretations of the Church.* Louisville, Ky.: Westminster John Knox, 1993.

Elisabeth Schüssler Fiorenza (1938–). Roman Catholic. Although most often noted for her contributions to biblical studies, Schüssler Fiorenza has contributed mightily to feminist theological work on hermeneutics, ecclesiology, liturgy, and a host of social issues.

- *In Memory of Her: A Feminist Theological Reconstruction of Christian Origins.* New York: Crossroad: 1983.
- *Discipleship of Equals: A Critical Feminist Ekklesialogy of Liberation.* New York: Crossroad, 1993.

African American Theologies

James H. Cone (1938–). African Methodist Episcopal. This American theologian is the architect of the Black Theology movement and author of many of its foundational works.

- *God of the Oppressed.* Rev. ed. Maryknoll, N.Y.: Orbis Books, 1997.
- *A Black Theology of Liberation.* 20th anniversary ed. Maryknoll, N.Y.: Orbis Books, 1990.
- *Martin and Malcolm and America: A Dream or a Nightmare?* Maryknoll, N.Y.: Orbis Books, 1991.

Martin Luther King Jr. (1929–1968). Baptist. The famed civil rights leader's theology emerged at the nexus of African American theologies and American personalist philosophy, as well as his activism.

- *Strength to Love.* Minneapolis: Fortress Press, 1981 [1963].
- *A Testament of Hope: The Essential Writings of Martin Luther King, Jr.* Ed. James M. Washington. San Francisco: Harper & Row, 1986.

Cornel West (1953–). Baptist. A leading voice in progressive Christian thought, West has combined prophetic African American insights with Continental philosophy.

- *Prophesy Deliverance! An Afro-American Revolutionary Christianity.* Philadelphia: Westminster Press, 1982.
- *Race Matters.* With a new preface. Boston: Beacon Press, 2001 [1993].

Delores S. Williams. Presbyterian. Theology written from the perspective of African American women is known as womanist theology. One of the most important works in womanist theology is that of Delores Williams, Paul Tillich Professor Emerita of Theology and Culture at Union Theological Seminary, New York City.

- *Sisters in the Wilderness: The Challenge of Womanist God-Talk.* Maryknoll, N.Y.: Orbis Books, 1993.

Hispanic/Latino Theologies

Orlando O. Espín (1947–). Roman Catholic. Espín's systematic theology draws specifically on patterns in popular religiosity.

- *The Faith of the People: Theological Reflections on Popular Catholicism.* Maryknoll, N.Y.: Orbis Books, 1997.

Justo L. González (1937–). Methodist. An influential biblical interpreter and historian of theology, Cuban American thinker González also penned the first explicitly Hispanic theology.

- *Christian Thought Revisited: Three Types of Theology.* Maryknoll, N.Y.: Orbis Books, 1999.
- *Mañana: Christian Theology from a Hispanic Perspective.* Nashville, Tenn: Abingdon Press, 1990.

Ada María Isasi-Díaz (1943–). Roman Catholic. Isasi-Díaz, born in Cuba and now teaching at the Theological School at Drew University, has developed a *mujerista* theology rooted in the experience of Hispanic women in the United States.

- *En la Lucha/In the Struggle: Elaborating a Mujerista Theology.* 10th anniversary ed. Minneapolis: Fortress Press, 2004.
- *Mujerista Theology: A Theology for the Twenty-First Century.* Maryknoll, N.Y.: Orbis Books, 1996.

Orthodox Theologies

Vladimir Lossky (1903–1958). Russian Orthodox. German-born Russian, Lossky taught in Paris and became a highly respected interpreter of the Orthodox tradition today.

- *The Mystical Theology of the Eastern Church.* Crestwood, N.Y.: St. Vladimir's Seminary Press, 2002).

John Meyendorff (1926–1992). Educated in Paris, Meyendorff came to the United States, taught at St. Vladimir's Orthodox Theological Seminary in New York, and penned important works in history and patristics as well as theology.

- *Byzantine Theology: Historical Trends and Doctrinal Themes.* 2nd ed. Bronx, N.Y.: Fordham University Press, 1983 [1979].

John D. Zizioulas (1931–). Widely discussed is his work on the Trinity from a contemporary Orthodox theological perspective.

- *Being as Communion: Studies in Personhood and the Church.* Crestwood, N.Y.: St. Vladimir's Seminary Press, 1985.

Glossary

anti-Semitism: prejudice against Jews.

apocalyptic: a view of history that claims that the events preceding the end of time have been revealed to one or more individuals in coded form.

apologetics: the theological movement concerned with the defense of Christian doctrine; based on the Greek *apologia,* meaning "in defense of."

Christian ethics: the discipline devoted to determining the proper conduct for Christians.

Christian realism: a theological movement that combines a rigorous social analysis with a commitment to achieve improved (although unlikely ideal) social conditions.

christology: literally, "the study of Christ"; addresses the identity of Jesus ("the person of Christ").

crucifixion: the death of Christ at Golgotha, or Calvary; from the Latin *crucifixio,* meaning "fixed to a cross."

dualism: the perspective that suggests that reality is divided into two categories (for example, light and darkness).

ecclesiology: the study of the church; from the Greek *ekklesia,* meaning "a calling out."

egalitarian: a view that regards all human beings as equals.

eschatological feminism: a term used by Rosemary Radford Ruether to refer to the belief that Christ restored the original fundamental equality between men and women.

eschatology: a study of the last things, such as afterlife and the end of human history.

eucharist: literally, "thanksgiving" (Greek, *eukharistia*); also known as *communion.*

exile: the captivity of the Jews in Babylon from 587 to 539 BCE.

faith: defined classically in Hebrews as "the assurance of things hoped for, the conviction of things not seen" (11:1).

feminism: a social movement that promotes gender equality and that corrects sexist understandings of the role of women.

gnosticism: a general perspective in the early church that claimed salvation was based on a secret knowledge (*gnosis*) possessed by the few.

hermeneutical theology: a theological movement engaged in the proper interpretation of scriptural and traditional claims.

Holocaust: the systematic murder and attempted extermination of the Jews by the Nazi regime of Adolf Hitler (1889–1945) and its collaborators (Hebrew, *Shoah*).

hypostatic union: the traditional expression describing the unity of Christ's human and divine natures.

imago Dei: literally, "the image of God" (Latin); the biblical claim that humans are created in God's image and hence have an essential equality and share in some imperfect way in God's nature.

incarnation: the belief that Christ was God in the flesh.

inclusivism: the perspective that other belief systems are valid for other individuals and worthy of respect, even if they conflict with one's own belief system.

liberalism: a theological movement committed to revising traditional Christian beliefs in light of evidence gathered in other academic disciplines.

liberation theology: a theological movement that understands the central biblical message to be one of freedom from economic, political, social, and spiritual oppression.

Logos: literally, "the Word" (Greek); a dynamic principle of structure and development inherent in God; according to the prologue of John's gospel, Christ is the incarnation of the Word in history.

Marxism: the political and economic philosophy of Karl Marx (1818–1883).

metaphorical theology: a theological movement that emphasizes the tentative, symbolic nature of human language about God.

myth: for the twentieth-century biblical theologian Rudolf Bultmann, a prescientific understanding of the world presumed in New Testament writings.

natural theology: a theological movement in which knowledge about God is based on observing the world, without referring to Scripture.

neo-Thomism: a theological movement of the late- nineteenth and early twentieth centuries based on interpretations of the philosophy and theology of Thomas Aquinas (1225–1274).

orthodoxy (or, being orthodox): literally, "correct belief" (Greek); holding the doctrines and beliefs established by a religious authority.

pacifism: a perspective based on the commitment to nonviolence.

parable: a short, allegorical story that teaches a moral lesson or truth; it generally involves a comparison between events in ordinary life and the nature of the kingdom of God.

pastoral: a ministerial approach concerned with the spiritual, psychological, and emotional needs of church members.

patriarchy: a social system in which women are subordinate to men.

patripassianism: the belief that the Father suffered along with the Son.

pietism: a form of theology and spirituality that emphasizes the heart or emotions as the center of religious experience.

pluralism: a perspective that recognizes the wide diversity of beliefs held by individuals and cultures around the world.

political theology: a theological movement of the mid-twentieth century that originated in western Europe and focused on the issues of nuclear proliferation and the politics of the Cold War.

postliberalism: a theological movement in which the claims are grounded in particular narratives, rather than universal systems.

praxis: literally, "action" or "practice" (Greek/Latin); engaging in God's liberating work in the world.

predestination: the belief that God has elected a certain number of persons for eternal salvation and damnation.

process theology: a theological movement based on the beliefs of Alfred North Whitehead (1861–1947) that suggests the relationship between God and the world is one of reciprocity.

proleptic: Wolfhart Pannenberg's preferred term for the anticipation generated by events such as the resurrection.

prophets: the biblical figures who delivered God's message to the people and often proclaimed God's imminent judgment against the people for failing to remain loyal to the covenant.

realism: a perspective that seeks approximations of justice in a sinful world.

reason: the human faculty that assesses claims of truth.

relativism: a perspective that suggests all claims are relative to or dependent on the culture or individual.

religion: from the Latin *religio*, meaning "respect for what is sacred," or *religare*, meaning "to bind fast"; a way of life lived in reference to a transcendent reality.

resurrection: the victory of Christ over the power of sin and death; the cornerstone of Christian faith.

revelation: an unveiling of God to the people; the means by which God's nature and intentions for the world are disclosed.

secular theology: a theological movement based on the assumption that traditional claims about God have become less relevant or less applicable in the modern age.

secularization: the social process whereby persons understand and interpret their lives without reference to God.

soteriology: literally, "the study of salvation"; an understanding of the nature of salvation and how Jesus brought it about by his life, death, and resurrection ("the work of Christ").

theological anthropology: the understanding of the human person from the perspective of a specific religious tradition.

theology: literally, "the study of God"; critical reflection on religious beliefs, doctrines, and practices.

transcendental Thomism: a theological movement that incorporates the criticisms and insights of the philosopher Immanuel Kant (1724–1804) with the theology of Thomas Aquinas (1225–1274); special attention is given to the conditions that make human knowledge possible.

trinity (or, trinitarian): the Christian view of God as one being in three persons: Father, Son, and Holy Spirit.

Index